Jack Fitzgerald

Three Centuries of Newfoundland Justice

The Hangman is Never Late

Dec '06

I thought of You
while I was
reading and fou d
this! love K

The Hangman is Never Late

Three Centuries of Newfoundland Justice

Jack Fitzgerald

St. John's, Newfoundland
1999

Le Conseil des Arts | The Canada Council
du Canada | for the Arts

We acknowledge the support of The Canada Council for the Arts for our publishing program.

We acknowledge the financial support of the Government of Canada through the Book Publishing Industry Development Program (BPIDP) for our publishing program.

Cover: Maurice Fitzgerald

∞ Printed on acid-free paper

Published by
CREATIVE PUBLISHERS
an imprint of CREATIVE BOOK PUBLISHING
a division of Creative Printers and Publishers Limited
a Print Atlantic associated company
P.O. Box 8660, St. John's, Newfoundland and Labrador A1B 3T7

4th Printing — August 2003

Printed in Canada by:
PRINT ATLANTIC

Canadian Cataloguing in Publication Data

Fitzgerald, Jack, 1945–
 The hangman is never late

ISBN 1-894294-02-5

 1. Crime — Newfoundland — History
 2. Criminals — Newfoundland — History.   I. Title
   HV6809.N5F583   1999   364.1'09718   C99-950117-8

I dedicate this book to my mother,
Bride (Evoy) Fitzgerald
who passed away in August, 1994.

Table of Contents

CHAPTER 4 — Early Twentieth Century

CHAPTER 5 — Later Twentieth Century

CHAPTER 6 — Justice Potpourri

Preface

The Hangman is Never Late covers three centuries of crime and justice in Newfoundland. Researching and gathering material for this book spanned several decades and presented quite a challenge. I encountered many problems in researching eighteenth and nineteenth century records. This problem stemmed from the fact that some of our historical records were destroyed in the several major fires which ravaged the City of St. John's. In addition, recorded events frequently omitted the first name of individuals or the positions they held. Because of these factors some items are very short, yet they merit inclusion in this book.

Records of twentieth century justice stories were easier to research. However, early in my work I discovered the unreliability of individual memories. In dealing with individuals and criminal offences it is especially important that records be accurate. For, example in one case popular belief held that a female murder victim had been sexually abused before dying. However, neither court records nor police reports contained any references to support that claim. I interviewed a member of the jury who insisted that evidence of the abuse was presented in court. Once again I reviewed the records and found nothing to support the sexual assault claim. Yet, the jury member insisted it had been presented in court, and went on to summarize the Pathologist's description of the act. Finally, I accessed the Pathologist report; and the medical report of a second doctor. The reports stated specifically that the victim had not been sexually abused. When I presented copies of these reports to the juror he concluded that he must have been influenced over the years by popular myth about the murder.

In another case, people I interviewed in connection with a St. John's murder stated that the female victim had been murdered by her enraged boyfriend because she was pregnant from another man. However, medical records I reviewed confirmed the girl was not pregnant. The Valdmanis story is another in which the public perception and some individual memories are at odds with the actual court evidence. Over the years speculation and rumours which were rampant at the time became the accepted version of the case rather than the actual truth.

Adding to the problem of getting accurate information is the factor that erroneous information regarding criminal stories sometimes appear in published records.In cases where living witnesses or media reports conflicted with police records and sworn evidence given in court, I choose to stick with the court records.

—*Jack Fitzgerald, May 1999*

FOREWORD
Hon. Edward Roberts, Q.C.
Former Newfoundland Justice Minister

Every Newfoundlander knows that our island home can boast of a history which stretches back many thousands of years, to the day the first aboriginal peoples made their way here from what is now mainland Canada. The Norse people lived here for a short few years at the turn of the first millennium, and western Europeans first settled Newfoundland at least 500 years ago. But while all of this is very familiar, most of us know remarkably little about the lives, the loves and the labours of the men and women who made their homes here, and from whom most present day Newfoundlanders are descended.

Jack Fitzgerald has written several books that go a long way towards helping us to relive our past. He is fascinated by the seamier side of our history, in part because tales of crime and criminals and derring-do are interesting in themselves, and in part because they reveal much about the way in which people lived, loved and worked in bygone days. This book is a worthy successor to the others he has written.

Mr. Fitzgerald is a meticulous researcher, who knows a colourful and important story when he reads about it. He is a fine writer and a vigourous raconteur, and has found a rich trove of treasure. Some of his tales are well-known, while others have long been shrouded by the mists of time.

And what stories there are to be told! They are all here. There is the 1797 mutiny, when Royal Navy seamen in St. John's challenged their officers in an echo of the Great Mutiny that bedeviled the Navy at its English bases in that year. Equally fascinating is the story of the threatened uprising, in 1800, by a group of the Irish who were members of the British

Army, and the tale of the last duel fought in Newfoundland, in 1825, when two idle and quarrelsome Army officers stood on the bank of Rennie's River in St. John's and fired pistols at each other. (The pistols are in the Newfoundland Museum's collection). Mr Fitzgerald recounts the story of the Flat Island moonshiners, which saw HMS *Cornwall* (with Joe Smallwood aboard) sent to Bonavista Bay to quell a tempest-in-a-teapot rebellion by a group of fishermen who enjoyed a drop of the good stuff, notwithstanding that it didn't come from the BLC. And there is still more — mass murder, forgery, the slaying of a politician, a World War II riot by disgruntled Royal Navy seamen in St. John's, and the tawdry tale of Alfred Valdmanis all find their place in this anthology.

The book's concluding chapter, entitled "Justice Potpourri," is just that. It's a collection of incidents describing some of the oddities and absurdities which are an inescapable part of any human endeavour as far reaching and as all-pervasive as a society's attempt to maintain law and order. The chapter will either reinforce one's faith in the English common law, notwithstanding its imperfections, or leave one convinced that we are not very far removed from the days when people lived in caves and might was right. It is a fitting finish to a delightful book, one which will be read with profit and pleasure by anybody with an interest in the long, colourful and fascinating story of Newfoundland.

Appreciation

Several people were most helpful to me in preparing this book for publication. I am especially grateful to Don Morgan of Creative Publishers for his enthusiasm and constructive support throughout my work. Also, a special thank you to Trudy Morgan-Cole, who edited the book and had some positive influence on its final presentation.

My friend, Richard (Dick) Hartery, who has helped me on several of my books was particularly helpful in getting *The Hangman is Never Late* ready for the publisher. Special thanks to my son Maurice for designing another appealing cover.

Chapter One

The Eighteenth Century

June, 1740
The Murdering Cobhams

Eric Cobham, a French magistrate, confessed his sins to a priest on his death bed, giving him a detailed written confession of his early life of crime. Cobham asked the priest to make certain it was published in full after his death. The priest carried out Cobham's wishes, but when the book was published, the magistrate's heirs travelled all over France buying up every available copy.

A single copy of that book survived, and although badly worn, it is preserved today in the national archives of France. It tells of an almost unbelievable life of crime by Cobham and his wife Marie, involving torture, mass murder and piracy in Newfoundland.

Although Cobham was a French magistrate, he was not French. He was born at Poole, England and by his late teens was involved in rum smuggling between England and France. On one trip, after landing ten thousand gallons of French Brandy at Poole, he was captured and imprisoned at the infamous Newgate Prison, where some of England's most gruesome executions took place. After being flogged, he served two years in prison before he was released at the age of twenty. He went to work as a clerk in an inn at Oxford, but he had learned little from his prison experience and found himself in trouble again after he robbed one of the inn guests of a bag of gold. Theft was a more serious offence than rum running; the penalty was execution by hanging. But Cobham managed to cast the blame on the Inn's owner, who was found guilty of the theft and hanged at Newgate.

Cobham's criminal mind planned to use his new found wealth to gain even more. He went to Plymouth, purchased a ship, recruited a crew and armed the vessel with fourteen guns. From Plymouth, Cobham launched his career as a pirate. His first act of piracy netted him forty thousand pounds sterling. It was common for eighteenth century pirates to be lenient towards prisoners, but Cobham was a ruthless and cruel man. After capturing and taking the gold from an East Indian ship, he scuttled it, and everyone on board was drowned.

When he returned to Plymouth he met and married a girl named Maria Lindsay. Maria enthusiastically joined Eric in his piracy. After they captured and scuttled another ship near New York, they sailed to Newfoundland where their piracy flourished and wealth grew. It was 1740 when the Cobhams set up headquarters at Sandy Point, Bonne Bay. Sandy Point at the time had no civil authority, and was only sparsely inhabited by Indians and a few fishermen from Acadia. From the protection of the snug harbour, the Cobhams were able to attack ships travelling to and from the Maritimes, mainland Canada and the French island colony of St. Pierre. Furs were as valuable as gold in those days, and the Cobhams captured many rich cargoes which they sold on the French black market.

The Cobhams went undetected for years because they murdered or tortured to death every person they captured. Shipowners believed their vessels had simply gone to the bottom of the Atlantic during severe storms. Maria Cobham surpassed her husband in the art of killing and mutilation. She often carved up the prisoners with her sword or had them tied to masts and practised pistol shooting at them, taking care to avoid killing them until a limb had been shot off. On one occasion she had an entire crew sewn alive into sacks and thrown overboard. Another time she set a captured West Indian crew at ease by inviting them to join her in the galley for lunch, then poisoned them by lacing their food with laudanum.

After twenty years of piracy the Cobham's had accumulated a magnificent fortune and selected France as a place to settle. They purchased a mansion and large estate from the Duc de Chartier at La Havre.

They owned a private harbour and a private yacht that were the envy of the French aristocracy. When the Cobhams became bored they sometimes used the yacht for brief flings of piracy. On one such escapade they captured a West Indian brig, massacred the crew and sold the ship at Bordeaux, France.

Impressed by the Cobham wealth, prominent French people used their influence to have Cobham appointed a judge in the French county courts. As the years passed, Maria slowly grew insane. One day she went to the cliffs near her estate, took laudanum and jumped over the cliffs to make doubly sure she would not survive.

Cobham lived for years afterwards and died a natural death. Following his death his family was elevated to the

French aristocracy. When the death bed confessions of Eric Cobham appeared in print the Cobham heirs quickly got them off the market. Some British merchants got hold of the confession, compared the details given by Cobham with their own records of the ships he captured, their crews, the dates and cargoes and were satisfied with the accuracy of the infamous Cobham Confession.

June 26, 1748

A Harbour Main Murder

*L*aurence Kneeves of Harbour Main ordered his friend John Kelly to drink a mug of flip. The suggestion resulted in an argument, a gruesome death for Kelly, and a most unusual punishment for Kneeves.

The term 'mug of flip' has long disappeared from usage in Newfoundland, but during the mid-eighteenth century it was quite common. Flip was a concoction of liquor, eggs and sugar which was used as a pep drink to give energy. To suggest or order someone 'to drink flip' was to accuse them of being lazy.

The tragic story of John Kelly took place at Harbour Main on Thursday, June 26, 1748. John Kelly and friend, John Cuddy, paid a friendly visit to the home of James Moores. Kneeves, an employee of Moores, was also at the house. As they were leaving, Kneeves called to Kelly, "Drink a mug of flip." This sparked an argument and before anyone knew what was happening, punches were being thrown between Kelly and Kneeves.

The fight moved outdoors and Cuddy made a move to

part the antagonists. Derby Callahan, a heavy set rowdy type individual, stepped in and warned that he would 'knock to the ground' any man who tried to stop the fight. Cuddy realized he couldn't handle Callahan so he left to seek help. When he returned the fight was over and Kelly was stretched out on his back. Cuddy asked, "Is he dead?" Kneeves, standing nearby with his hands covered in blood, said, "No, he's just drunk. I'll throw some water in his face." There was no response. Kneeves realized then that Kelly was dead.

There were no doctors in the area to perform an examination of the victim. In place of this, a group of private citizens viewed the body and gave a sworn account of their findings to George Garland, the Justice of the Peace at Harbour Grace. The witnesses included John Moore, Roger Benlite, John Woodford, Thomas Balaine, William Brown, Pearce Butler and Philip Enough.

They gave a combined statement which read: "By all first circumstances and appearances found, John Kelly was barbarously murdered and abused, his head being battered severely and his handkerchief so tight around his neck that it was impossible to put a knife between the flesh and handkerchief."

Kneeve's trial took place at the court house in St. John's. When all evidence had been presented, the judge gave the jury an opportunity to ask questions. He then ordered the bailiff, "to keep the jury without meat, drink, fire, candle or lodging or suffering any person to speak to them until they are agreed on their verdict." The jury was back with its verdict in ninety minutes. They found Kneeves guilty of manslaughter.

Punishment was swift in those days. The judge ordered that the following day at noon, Kneeves be brought back into the courtroom and branded on the right hand with a hot iron marked with the letter 'R'. In addition he was ordered to forfeit all his goods and chattels, and then banished from the country.

It was customary that a person sentenced to banishment during this period be placed on the first available boat leaving the country. Because of this there was no mention of the place of banishment. The 'R' was used to mark a person who had committed murder or a repeat offender.

July 6, 1752

Murder at Fermeuse

The appearance of William Murphy of Fermeuse in Court at St. John's on a charge of murder presented an unusual problem for the Court. Murphy and several witnesses were all Irish immigrants. They spoke only Irish (Gaelic) and none of them understood a word of English. Fortunately, the problem was solved when the Court obtained the services of a St. John's Irishman named Edward Corkeran who spoke fluent English and who graciously consented to act as interpreter.

Bill Murphy's ordeal with the law began during the afternoon of July 6, 1752 when he became involved in an argument with two fellow Irishmen over the best way to clean fish. Murphy, along with his two cohorts Billy Quinn and Jimmy Bryane, were employed by Maurice Hoggathee, a successful Fermeuse fisherman.

The three were busy cleaning fish on Hoggathee's Wharf and were chatting with each other when Quinn suddenly began to criticize the way Murphy and Bryane were cleaning fish. Both Quinn and Murphy were proud and hot-tempered Irishmen, but Bryane was a quiet man and was not offended by Quinn's comments. Murphy on the other hand was quick to point out to Quinn that he could clean fish better and faster than him anytime, even with one hand held behind his back.

Bryane giggled at Murphy's remark as he continued gutting the fish. This hurt Quinn's pride and he grabbed the biggest cod fish he could lay his hands on and belted Murphy across the face. Murphy then grabbed a fish and delivered a counter-blow to Quinn's face. At this point the combatants stood up facing each other ready for a skirmish.

Quinn seized a second cod. Now armed with two fish, he circled Murphy. Not wanting to fight handicapped, Murphy grabbed two fish and the battle started with each Irishman clobbering the other with fish.

Jimmy Bryane attempted to break up the fight but got hit in the face with a fish. This distracted Murphy and allowed Quinn to replace his fish with a mop handle. He then started to batter Murphy over the head with the mop. When Murphy dropped to the ground Quinn ran from the wharf claiming he was going to Hoggathee to report the others for doing sloppy work.

When Murphy regained his composure he seized a five foot longer* and hid behind the gate to the wharf awaiting Quinn's return. True to his word, Quinn complained to his employer about the others and was told to return to the wharf. Hoggathee promised he would come down to the wharf within an hour to tend to the matter.

Hearing Quinn approach the gate, Murphy braced him-

---

* A length of small tree trunk, used for fence rails and fish stage construction

self with the longer held over his head ready for action. Just as Quinn stepped triumphantly onto the fishing stage Murphy delivered two hard clouts onto Quinn's head. Quinn keeled over and lay motionless on the wharf.

Satisfied that he had evened the score, Murphy took his place alongside of Bryane and the two resumed their work of cleaning fish. About an hour later one of Hoggathee's salters went up to the master and told him Quinn was dead. Hoggathee rushed to the wharf and saw the body of Quinn in a pool of blood by the stage door. Dr. George Bryane was called in. After examining the victim he confirmed that Quinn was dead. The matter was turned over to the Justice of the Peace who had Murphy arrested.

On September 2, 1752, Murphy stood before the bar of the Court in St. John's and through the Irish interpreter Corkeran was asked, "Are you guilty or not guilty?" Murphy replied, "Not guilty."

"How do you wish to be tried?" asked the judge through the interpreter. Murphy responded, "By God and my country."

James Bryane, Maurice Hoggathee and Dr. George Bryane were called as witnesses and were sworn in by the Court. The administration of the oath was referred to as swearing on the Holy Evangelists. Members of the Grand Jury which indicted Murphy included: William Keene, Michael Gill, John de Grave, George Oliver, James Escott, Edward Cahill and George Stancombe.

The indictment read as follows

The jurors of our sovereign Lord the King, upon Oath, present William Murphy of the Kingdom of Ireland, fisherman, not having God before his eyes, but being moved and seduced by the instigation of the devil on the sixth of July in the 26th year of the reign of our Sovereign Lord, George the Second, by the grace of

God of Great Britain, France and Ireland, King, Defender of the Faith, did sometime in the evening of the said day at Fermouze Harbour, as appears before us by force and arms, did make an assault in and upon the body of one William Quinn, upon his head, two blows with the end of a longer of about five feet which made a wound on the forehead over the left eye of which wound it is imagined William Quinn died of.

The trial lasted only part of the day and the jury was back with verdict by 3:00 pm. The verdict was guilty as charged. The judge asked Murphy if he had any reason as to why the death penalty should not be imposed. Murphy responded with a petition to the Court requesting that the penalty of transportation be imposed instead of hanging and asking for the mercy of the Court.*

The judge briefly considered the request then pronounced the following sentence: "That you William Murphy shall be returned to the gaol from whence you came and from there to the place of execution where you are to be hanged by the neck until you shall be dead, dead, dead and the Lord have mercy on your soul."

Years later, oral folklore along the Southern Shore quoted the judge as commenting: "William Murphy...the morning of September 15 will likely be a bright clear sunny day. No doubt a gentle breeze will sweep down over the Southside Hills refreshing everyone it touches. The men of the city will be tending to their work on the Waterfront or harvesting the fields, the women of this fair city will be cleaning house or preparing food for the day. It will be a glorious September day in every way....but you William Murphy, you rotten

---

* Transportation meant being deported out of the country and was a penalty under the law.

bastard will see none of this...because I sentence you to hang at 5:30 am."

September 9, 1754

Court Judge Murdered

The Power Gang of Freshwater Bay shocked the inhabitants of the Island of Newfoundland on the night of Monday, September 9, 1754 when, during a commando-type robbery attempt, they murdered a very prominent Newfoundland Court Justice named William Kean. The mastermind and leader of the gang was a Freshwater Bay woman named Eleanor Power. Eleanor, with the aid of her husband, put together a gang of ten members, including herself and husband. Their aim was to steal the fortune they believed to be hidden inside Judge Kean's summer home at Quidi Vidi.

The Power Gang included four soldiers from the St. John's Garrison: Edmund McGuire, Dennis Hawkins, John Munhall, and John Moody. The remaining four were from Freshwater Bay: Nicholas Tobin, Paul McDonald, Matthew Halleran and Lawrence Lamley.

Power offered each gang member a three thousand dollar share of the loot. One member of the group, Edmund McGuire, was motivated by revenge. He felt the Judge had wronged him in the past when he was tried in Kean's court. Each participant had to swear on a prayer book to be true to each other.

The first attempt to pull off the caper failed when the group arrived at the scene only to find that Kean's son and some neighbours were working outside in the area. For the second attempt Eleanor dressed in men's clothing and led the group aboard a skiff which sailed from Freshwater Bay to King's Wharf in St. John's Harbour. From there they went on foot to Kean's summer home. When they arrived at the scene the house was in darkness. They forced entry and removed a large chest which they thought contained the treasure. They also pocketed some of Kean's silverware when leaving.

Gang members carted the chest into a wooded area and broke it open expecting to find the money, but to their dismay, the only thing inside were several bottles of liquor. Disappointed and concerned over the consequences of their deed some of the men wanted to give up and go home. John Munhall had other ideas. He raised his musket and warned that he would kill anyone trying to leave.

Eleanor then led another attempt to find the money. She sent four men to make sure neighbours wouldn't interfere in the robbery. Richard Power and Moody guarded the servants in the kitchen while Eleanor and Lamley hid in the woods outside. Halleran and McGuire went upstairs to Kean's room. When they removed a large box from beneath Kean's bed, Kean woke and cried out,"Murder! Murder!" Halleran put a quilt over Kean to keep him quiet, but he managed to jump up and with his fingers he doused the candle in McGuire's hand. He then grabbed Halleran by the leg. Halleran struck Kean with a scythe and McGuire hit the judge with the butt end of a musket.

Citizens of St. John's were outraged next morning when they learned of the murder of Judge Kean. Nick Tobin, one of the gang members, fearing the consequences of their deed, went to authorities and made a deal that led to the conviction of the others.

The trial was held on October 8, 1754. Medical evidence showed that the Judge had been killed by wounds inflicted with the gun butt and scythe. In court, Eleanor and Richard Power had nothing to say in their defence. The others argued that they helped with the robbery but not the murder. All except Tobin were convicted and sentenced to be hanged. McGuire and Halleran, who had actually killed the Judge, had the added sentence of gibbeting.

The gang was then escorted from the court room. The military members were imprisoned at the Garrison in St. John's, while the civilian members were held on board the HMS *Penzance* which was harboured near Kean's Wharf. The gang had been divided because of security concerns. Governor Hugh Bonfoy later pardoned Lamley, McDonald, Moody, Munhall and Hawkins.

At noon on October 10, Halleran and McGuire were taken to the gallows on Kean's Wharf and the sentence of the Court was carried out. At noon the following day Eleanor and Richard Power looked out over the St. John's Harbour for the last time. They were hanged from the same gallows on Kean's Wharf. The bodies of Halleran and McGuire were left hanging in chains on public display for a week after the hangings. The bodies of all four were buried near the gallows, which is now the site of Royal Trust Building on Water Street.

April 17, 1759

Hanged For Killing A Cow

William Gilmore carried on a thriving business in his Quidi Vidi home selling liquor to soldiers from the garrison in St. John's. On April 17,1759, while entertaining a few friends in his home, Gilmore suggested that they steal and kill a cow. He offered to assist them by hiding the meat and helping cover up the deed. David Williams and Richard Sutley listened to Gilmore's suggestion but didn't take it seriously. In those days this type of crime was punishable by hanging and the two were not willing to risk their lives for a meal of beef.

Gilmore, however, was determined to get that fresh meat and as the evening wore on and the drinking continued he finally persuaded his two friends that the deed could be carried out without anyone being caught. At one point he said, "If I was well I'd go myself and kill a cow, a calf and a stag. There's no need for anyone to find out. I'll hide the meat."

Gilmore provided Williams and Sutley with a Dutch knife and a hatchet and off they went to do Gilmore's bidding. They searched an area known as the 'Barrens' which was located in the area now occupied by Bannerman Park and Government House. Coming upon a cow grazing in the area, Williams raised the axe above his head and struck the cow. When they were sure it was dead the two proceeded to skin it and cut it up.

Meanwhile, Gilmore, in preparation for the pending arrival of fresh meat, told his wife to clean out the pot. Margaret Gilmore replied, "I certainly will not. There's a full pot of chowder in that pot and we're having that for supper." Gilmore then insisted she clean out the pot, explaining that he had some friends coming to supper and he wanted something nice to serve.

When Williams and Sutley arrived with the meat Gilmore helped them hide it in the well. When his wife realized what was happening she began to scream, "You are harbouring thieves. You are disgracing me!" To quieten her down

Gilmore lifted his leg and kicked her in the stomach, calling her "a foolish bitch."

The following morning a man named James Forrester arrived at the Gilmore home. He showed Mrs. Gilmore a knife and asked who owned it. She didn't hesitate. "That looks very much like mine, but I'm not sure. My husband should know; wait here and I'll get him." When Gilmore came into the kitchen he identified the knife as his. He said, "If that knife killed twenty cows, it's still my knife."

Gilmore, Sutley and Williams were arrested and brought to trial. The trial got underway in Court at St. John's on September 11, 1759. The indictment charging the three read in part,

> ...not having God before their eyes and moved and seduced by the instigation of the devil on the 17 day of April, 1759, at St. John's did feloniously, willfully and of malice forethought seize on and kill a certain cow grazing in the barrens of St. John's.

The trial held before a twelve man jury only took a few hours and the jury took only fifteen minutes to return a guilty verdict. Gilmore was executed by hanging. The records are not clear on what happened to Sutley and Williams.

December 31, 1792

On December 31, 1792, Andrew Furlong was given an unusual punishment for stealing one gallon of rum from the Ferryland store of Richard Tydell. Furlong pleaded guilty and was sentenced to seventy-two lashes on the bare back.

The punishment involved taking the prisoner to several areas of Ferryland and partially administering the lashes in each area so all the population would have a chance to witness justice being done. He was first taken to the north side of Ferryland Harbour and tied to a post. Then twenty-four lashes were administered. The same was carried out on the southside of the harbour and the final lashes were given in front of the Ferryland Court House.

In addition the sentence required that Furlong be held in prison until he could be put aboard a ship leaving the country. He was banished and warned never to return to Newfoundland.

October 28, 1794

A Harbourfront Murder

Three companies of Newfoundland volunteer servicemen, the entire crews of six British Man o' War's, and crowds of city residents gathered at the St. John's waterfront on the morning of October 28, 1794 to witness one of the most unusual funerals in our history. The silence of that morning was broken by the steady and morbid beating of military drums along the shoreline as a flotilla of dories moved in a funeral procession on the harbour water. This unusual funeral was being held to honour the slain Lieutenant Richard Lawry, who had been killed several days before during an ambush by a group of city Irishmen.

Earlier on that fatal day Lawry was going about his regular routine as an officer on the H.M.S. *Boston*. The ship's captain was in a quandary over what to do about getting fourteen additional crew members needed to complete a cargo delivery to Portugal and Spain. On the previous day, he had made an unsuccessful attempt to recruit crew members from among the city's population. He was now being advised by captains from other ships to use his right to impress men into service. Reluctantly, the captain gave orders for Lawry and some crew members of the *Boston* to go ashore and impress the needed men for duty.

As Lawry led his press gang ashore in a large dory, two local Irishmen, Richard Power and Garret Farrell were just leaving a pub on Water Street to head home. A short while later the paths of Lawry and the two Irishmen crossed and the result was tragedy for all concerned. Lawry's group took the Irishmen by surprise and forced them, along with twelve others from the city, to accompany him aboard the *Boston*.

The following morning, six of the impressed men were released to their employers who exercised their right to claim employees. Although the Irish duo were employed by a Water Street merchant named Noble, their employer did not come to get them. The devious minds of the two were already at work to find a way to get out of their predicament, however. They joined with the other six in pledging to the captain their willingness to join His Majesty's Service. After making this commitment they asked the captain's permission to go ashore to pick up some pay due from their employer and to get their clothing.

The captain did not trust them so he assigned Lieutenant Lawry and four others to escort the two to their destination and then bring them back to the ship.

Lawry's group rowed ashore in a large dory and tied up at a wharf located at the upper end of the harbour. As they walked beneath a fish-flake they were ambushed by a group of Irishmen armed with wattels.* During the scuffle, Lawry

---

*   sticks

was beaten unconscious and two other crew members were seriously injured; one received minor cuts; the fourth escaped in the dory.

Evidence later showed that Power and Farrell played a major part in the attack upon Lawry. To throw suspicion away from themselves they brought the unconscious Lawry and his shipmates back to the captain of the *Boston* with the sad tale of how they were brutally attacked. Lawry passed away the following morning October 25. On the morning of Lawry's death, Newfoundland's Governor Sir James Wallace was on board H.M.S. *Monarch*, preparing for his departure for England. At that time the Governor would spend the winter months in England and return to govern the colony again in the spring. News of the attack on Lawry and his subsequent death distressed the Governor. He was concerned that if the culprits were not apprehended and justice quickly applied, riots and violence would erupt. If he left without dealing with the situation, a trial would be delayed until his return in the spring. The Governor felt that the trial and execution of the guilty was absolutely necessary in order to preserve good order.

All crew members of the British ships in port were ordered ashore to seek out evidence relating to the attack and murder of Lawry. Over one hundred city residents were rounded up, taken aboard the British vessels and questioned. This effort paid off and one Irishman who had been present at the beating of Lawry offered to give King's evidence in return for immunity against prosecution. The deal was made and, within hours, Power and Farrell were arrested and charged with murder.

The trial and execution were swift. Power and Farrell were tried on Wednesday, sentenced on Thursday and hanged on Friday. The hangings took place on October 31,

1794 at the Barrens near Fort Townshend. The executioner, wearing a long black cape, face mask and a wig made of black sheep's wool, appeared evil and intimidating as he walked towards the scaffold.

The condemned men were escorted to the gallows each wearing a turban made of three to four yards of white linen. Following the hangings their bodies were passed over to local surgeons for dissection.

The coffin for Lawry had been constructed by a ship's carpenter. It was draped with the British Flag, Lawry's uniform, his hat and sword. The coffin was lowered from the *Boston* into a dory as dories from the British ships *Monarch, Amphion, Pluto, Bonette, Lutane* and several local vessels, formed an escort for the funeral procession. As the procession moved slowly in a circular fashion around the harbour, other small boats joined in. The procession ended at the King's Wharf where hundreds of military and local people waited to accompany Lawry to his final resting place.

As the drums beat out the death watch, the coffin was removed from the dory and placed aboard a horse-drawn carriage. The funeral procession then made its way to the Church of England Cemetery on Duckworth Street, opposite where our courthouse now stands. There Lawry was laid to rest.

Before departing for England governor Wallace offered a fifty pound reward for information leading to the capture of William Barrows, who also took part in the murder of Lawry. A pardon was offered to anyone involved in the attack who would provide additional information on the murder. The condition for the pardon was that the informant had not struck Lawry and that the informant come forward within three months after the posting of the pardon notice. There is no evidence that the effort was successful and history records

Farrell and Power as the two who suffered the final penalty for Lawry's murder.

August 3, 1797

Mutiny at St. John's

Newfoundland criminal history is sprinkled with many strange, bizarre and unusual crimes. One such story involves mutiny aboard the HMS *Latona* in St. John's harbour on August 3rd, 1797.

At this time there was a universal spirit of mutiny throughout Britain. Dissidents openly challenged the authority of the Government, and many successful and unsuccessful mutinies occurred. One of the ring leaders of the dissidents in Britain was a man named Parker.

On August 3, 1797, some crew-members on board the *Latona*, loyal to Parker, refused to go aloft in a body and demanded to be put in irons. The *Latona*'s Captain Sotherton moved to squelch the mutiny by arresting the ringleader and ordering his punishment. The crewmembers tried to save their leader by demanding that he should not be punished. Sotherton ordered his marines to surround the men and draw their bayonets. In their rush to retreat, some of the men accidentally cut themselves on the bayonets.

With the crew under control, the ringleader was stripped to the waist and whipped. The men were angry. One marine guarding the men said, "The language of the seamen in their hammocks was terrible. They promised bloody work and threatened to throw the marines overboard as soon as the ship was in blue water."

Although released to go ashore several days later, the men were still discontented, and they attempted to incite the garrison. This outraged the citizens of St. John's. On September 6, Newfoundland Governor William Waldegrave received word from England that mutiny and rebellion had ended and Parker had been hanged for treason. The Governor, accompanied by marines from the Royal Artillery and a company from the Royal Newfoundland Regiment, went to the waterfront to address the British seamen in port.

He told them, "I'm happy to have this opportunity to thank you in person for your gallant and steady behaviour in support of your officers. You have shown yourselves to be good soldiers and true and faithful to your King and Country. There is not a person in St. John's but feels a regard and esteem for you. While I am sorry to say that they look on the seamen of the *Latona* with equal horror and detestation and indeed it is impossible that they should do otherwise, considering the infamy of their conduct, both on shore and afloat."

Addressing the *Latona* crew directly, Waldegrave continued, "But If I am to judge from your conduct, I must think that the majority of you are either villains or cowards. If the greater number of you are against your officers and refuse to obey their lawful commands, I have a right to say that you are traitors to your King and Country. If there are only a few bad men among you, which you presented to be the case, I maintain that you are a set of dastardly cowards for suffering yourselves to be bullied by a few villains who wish for nothing better than to see us become slaves of France.

"You were all eager for news and newspapers to see how your great delegate Parker was doing. I thank God, I have the satisfaction to inform you that he is hanged with many other of his atrocious companions. You looked up to him as example whilst he was in his glory. I recommend you look to his end as an example also. You may now indeed reap the advantage from contempt of the conduct of the vile incendiary."

Waldegrave then ordered his officers to kill instantly any sailor attempting to incite a mutiny. He also ordered the officers commanding the batteries at the entrance to St. John's harbour, "...to burn the *Latona* with red hot shot if there were any further signs of mutiny."

He explained, "I know in this case the officers must perish with you, but there is not one of them but is ready to sacrifice himself for the good of his country, in any mode whatsoever."

The Governor then ordered the mutineers, "...to go into church and pray to acquire the respect and love of their countrymen and eternal happiness in the next world."

The *Latona* incident created a great deal of fear and mistrust among the military. Officers of the Royal Newfoundland Regiment offered twenty guineas for the capture of any person spreading false rumours about their loyalty. The non-commissioned officers offered thirty guineas and the officers of the *Latona* added another twenty guineas for the same purpose. A short while later the *Latona* left St. John's and all talk of rebellion and mutiny left with it.

Chapter Two

Early Nineteenth Century

April 20, 1800
Treason in St. John's

The political situation in Newfoundland during 1800 was explosive. Fanned by reports that the British had suffered a series of defeats in Europe, and by the abolition of the Irish Parliament, a group of Irish military men at Fort William developed a plan to take control of the fort and the city of St. John's.

The conspirators planned to lead an uprising on April 20 during Sunday Mass; then proceed to the Protestant Church to take prisoner all the officers and leading inhabitants. Roman Catholic Archbishop, J. Louis O'Donel, an Irishman himself, had little sympathy for the Irish rebels and felt their violent activities back in Ireland were a disgrace to the Catholic Church. O'Donel learned of the plot and advised Brigadier General Skerrett, the commanding officer of the fort. When Sunday arrived the general foiled the planned rebellion by sending the men on manoeuvres, instead of the usual church parade.

This action served only to delay rebel plans, and, on the night of April 24, about twenty of them deserted their regiments and assembled at a powder shed on the barrens, Others from the fort were prevented from joining them after an alarm was raised at the fort. Two days later, the rebels confronted loyal troops in the woods near St. John's.

The troops overpowered them and the rebels scattered in an escape attempt. The troops managed to capture and arrest eight of the rebels. All were tried and convicted of treason. After receiving the death penalty they were marched to Gibbet Hill near Cabot Tower and executed. Following their execution, the eight men were left hanging in chains as a spectacle and deterrent to others who might consider rebellion.

There was strong support for the rebels among the people of St. John's, most of whom were Irish. The incident sparked United Irish support around the island, and Skerrett had to reinforce the garrison at Placentia. O'Donel's role in foiling the uprising is disputed by some historians. However, they acknowledge the strong possibility that he did play an important part by calming the civilian population and diminishing rebel support among the population and troops.

September 1, 1804
Murder on Southside Road

Catherine Brown, a young housewife of Southside Road, St. John's, and Richard Nickells, an agent with the firm of Thomas Row, also of the city, appeared before the same judge at the same time. Each was sentenced to hang.

Mrs. Brown went to the gallows when she was found guilty of the shooting death of her husband, John Brown. Nickells was to take the ten steps to the gallows because of forgery of a note valued at less than eighty dollars.

In Court, Nickells explained that he did not forge the note. He told the Court that when he discovered it was a forgery and looked into the matter he discovered that Catherine Brown and her husband had participated in the forgery. Aware of the serious penalty for such a criminal deed, Nickells gallantly took responsibility for the note, feeling that his employer would be sympathetic and allow him to repay the money. He told the judge, "I'd rather pay the money myself than to see anyone hurt."

His boss, however, was not so valiant and he pressed charges against Nickells. Nickells' brave effort to save Brown was useless. In an unrelated incident shortly after, Catherine Brown was arrested, charged and found guilty of the shooting death of her husband John Brown. After shooting him she set fire to the bedclothes and ran out onto Southside Road screaming, "John has shot himself, my God help me!"

The police investigation showed Mrs. Brown had somehow gotten hold of a pistol owned by next door neighbour George Whitten. Whitten told the police he discovered the weapon missing about three days before the murder. On the night of the murder, Mrs. Brown asked Hannah Whitten, George's sister, if she could borrow a tablespoon of gunpowder. She explained her husband needed it in order to kill a dog.

She might have gotten away with murder if she had not confided her secret to George Whitten. On the morning of the murder she told Whitten she had shot John and now she didn't know what to do. She said she was thinking of running away or drowning herself. Whitten's only reply to her was, "Then there will be two dead instead of one."

Whitten's evidence of this conversation along with Hannah's testimony concerning the gunpowder was enough to convince the jury to return with a guilty verdict.

As fate would have it, Nickells, who tried to save Mrs. Brown from the gallows by taking the rap on a forgery charge, now stood with her before the judge of the Court of Assizes. Both had been pronounced guilty of their respective charges. The whole matter had gotten out of hand for Nickells and he took advantage of the judge's invitation to give the Court any reasons as to why the death sentence should not be given them. Nickells repeated his claim of innocence and stated he was trying to save Brown from hanging. Catherine Brown remained silent.

On August 23, 1804, both Brown and Nickells were sentenced to hang. The hanging was to take place on Monday, August 27, 1804. Because of the circumstances of Nickells' case, the Governor commuted the death sentence to life in prison. Catherine Brown was hanged September 1, 1804.

Murderer With a Conscience

Mike Wilson of St. John's was found dead on December 27, 1848, near Military Road. He had been murdered by a blow to the head with a heavy object. An investigation carried out by police failed to turn up any evidence and the case remained unsolved for almost a year.

In August, 1849, the brigantine *Star* set sail from St. John's Harbour with a new crew member on board named Isaac

O'Neill. As the ship sailed along the coast, the captain noticed O'Neill's strange behaviour. O'Neill was depressed, avoided people and had lost his appetite. When questioned by the captain, he began sobbing and admitted to killing Wilson with a club.

Even though he was comforted by the captain, Wilson's murder continued to play heavily on O'Neill's mind. While on watch the following night, he jumped overboard. A rescue boat was launched from the *Star* but O'Neill swam away from it. He turned, waved to his would-be rescuers and disappeared beneath the deep waters.

1873

What ever Happened to Mary James?

Mary James was an eleven-year-old St. John's girl. Her father died when she was an infant, and Annie Walsh, a friend of the child's family, offered to take the child and rear her as her own. The mother agreed and after turning young Mary over to Annie Walsh, left Newfoundland to live and work on the mainland. Described by neighbours as a pretty, energetic and friendly child, Mary James disappeared during the year 1873 and was never heard from again.

Although Mary had been baptized an Anglican, the faith of her parents, Mrs. Walsh reared her as a Roman Catholic. Little Mary was very happy with the Walsh's and no one bothered the family until Mary turned eleven. Then turmoil and heartbreak struck the Walsh family.

Reverend M. Johnson, acting on behalf of the Anglican Church in St. John's, claimed the child. He was concerned that Mary was not being brought up in the faith which she had been baptized.

A court trial ensued which the local media dubbed, "The Ginx's Baby Trial." Mrs. Walsh refused to give up the child, and when authorities went to get Mary, she couldn't be found. Mrs. Walsh was brought back to court and ordered to disclose the whereabouts of the missing child. When she refused to do so, she was sentenced to the Penitentiary for contempt.

After serving a brief period in prison, Annie Walsh was released. She never did tell what happened to Mary James, and the child was never heard from again.

August 3, 1805
Child Murdered at Harbour Grace

@FIRST PARA = Jane Deay was born out of wedlock to James Conway and thirty-five-year-old Elizabeth Deay. Although Conway admitted to being the father, he never married Elizabeth and showed little affection for the child.

Elizabeth continued to see Conway, and the child was the source of bitter arguments between the two. In July, 1805, Elizabeth walked into the kitchen of Conway's home as he was eating breakfast. She laid the ten-month-old baby on the floor and announced that since he was the father he should look after it. Conway became angry and ordered her to take the child out of the house. She became frightened and did as he commanded. About an hour later as she sat on a grassy bank near Conway's home, he came along and forcibly took the child. She later told the Court that he didn't hit her but when he disappeared into the woods with the child she heard the infant scream 'dreadfully.'

She then enlisted the help of relatives and friends in searching for the child but the effort was of no avail. When she met Conway a couple of weeks later she asked what he had done with the child. He replied that he had taken her to the nurse at Bay Roberts to look after. She accused him of lying and suggested the child was dead.

Meanwhile, rumours spread around the community that little Jane was at the home of Mark Delaney in Bay Roberts. Elizabeth went to Delaney's but he told her he had never seen the child nor had he spoken with Conway. Delaney contacted Conway and told him he should let the mother know where the child was because she was terribly upset.

Conway said he would not give her that satisfaction but warned that if she continued to ask questions he would kill her and the child. Meanwhile, searchers discovered the body of the child in a wooded area. Her head had been kicked and there was evidence she had been beaten. Conway was arrested.

In his defence, Conway told the Court that, "The screams of the child when I took her were not unusual, for an infant just taken away from its mother will cry." He said at the time he was confused and upset and in a hurry to return to work, so he laid the child down in the woods, intending to return for her later. He claimed he didn't beat her and said he didn't go back because he was scared by the people in the woods looking for the child.

The Court had no mercy for Conway and he was sentenced to hang on August 3, 1805.

September 13, 1809

Edward Jordan Hanged

Edward Jordan's pathway into the history of the gallows in Canada began on September 13, 1809 when he took his wife Margaret and their four children on the schooner *Eliza* for a trip from Quebec to Halifax. Jordan, a passenger on the *Eliza*, was actually a fishing skipper, who operated out of the tiny fishing settlement called Perce on the Gaspe Peninsula.

After sharing a few drinks of grog with the ship's mate John Kelly, Jordan suggested that together they could jump the crew, take the ship and become rich men. Kelly agreed and the two involved Margaret Jordan in their plot to overpower Captain John Stairs and his crew. That night as the *Eliza* sailed peacefully between White Head and Cape Canso, Nova Scotia, the trio cornered Captain Stairs alone and beat him until he was almost unconscious. He would certainly have been killed if it had not been for the intercession of crewmen Ben Matthews and Tom Heath.

Matthews and Heath fought the three pirates long enough to draw their attack away from the Captain. However, they were no match for Jordan and Kelly, who after beating them senseless, tossed them overboard to drown. Then they went to pick up the Captain to consign him to the same fate, but they discovered he had escaped. Stairs had tossed a hatch overboard and jumped into the waters where he pulled himself onto the hatch.

When Jordan saw the Captain on the hatch he pulled his gun and began firing. Kelly ordered him to "put the gun away, he's a dead man, anyway." Jordan agreed observing that Stairs would certainly drown before morning. This error of judgement proved to be costly for Jordan. Stairs drifted for several hours and was rescued at dawn by a passing American schooner which was sailing to Boston.

At Boston he was given medical attention and he informed police that two of his crewmen had been murdered and his ship taken over by Jordan and Kelly. Both American and Canadian coastguards were alerted and a massive effort was made to locate the *Eliza* and bring the pirates to justice.

While this manhunt was taking place, Jordan was sailing along the south coast of Newfoundland in the Fortune Bay area, trying to recruit crew members for a planned Atlantic crossing to Ireland. At Little Bay West near Harbour Breton he tried to enlist Bill Carew and John Pigot for the *Eliza*. The two men went on board but refused to join the crew. They became suspicious after noticing the missing hatch, the fish not properly stowed and only two men, a woman and four children on board.

Kelly went to Harbour Breton and sought the help of the Magistrate there in getting seamen to work on the *Eliza*. The Magistrate, impressed by Kelly's presentation of the dire need for crew to help on the *Eliza*, had John Pigot summoned before him. The magistrate ordered that Pigot, who was unemployed, must sign on the *Eliza* or he would have him flogged in public. Pigot felt there was no other choice, so he reluctantly gathered his belongings and went on board the schooner.

Jordan continued his efforts to recruit seamen at St. Mary's Bay and along the Southern Shore. A man named John Power heard that the *Eliza* was going to Ireland and that the Captain was looking for a navigator. Power applied for the job and was hired at a monthly salary of eleven pounds sterling, considered good wages at the time. Four others signed on and by the time the ship set sail across the Atlantic it had six crew members from Newfoundland.

At sea a fight erupted between Jordan and Kelly over Jordan's wife. Jordan had discovered his wife sleeping with Kelly and attempted to shoot him. He would have succeeded had not Power intervened.

Knowing how treacherous Jordan was, Kelly slipped over the side that night with one of the ship's rowboats, and went ashore. What happened to him was never determined and he was never heard from again. Some say he settled on the Southern Shore and his descendants continue to live there.

Hot on the trail of the *Eliza* was the Canadian coastguard schooner *Cattle*, which finally caught up with her on the Atlantic. Jordan firmly believed Captain Stairs was dead, and tried to deceive the coastguard captain by claiming he was heading for Halifax. Jordan was shocked when the captain produced a warrant for the arrest of the ship and all those on board. The six Newfoundlanders had no idea why they were being arrested. Several coastguard crew members took control and brought the ship into Halifax Harbour.

An investigation at Halifax cleared the Newfoundlanders, who were released but kept at Halifax to participate as witnesses in the trials of Margaret and Edward Jordan. Although there was overwhelming evidence sufficient to convict Margaret Jordan, the Crown acquitted her on the ground that it would be shameful to leave her four children without a mother.

Edward Jordan, however, was found guilty of piracy and hanged at Halifax Harbour on November 20, 1809. His body was covered with pitch to preserve it and left hanging on the British Naval Gibbet until it was eventually washed out to sea during a severe winter storm.

While some historians claim Jordan was the last person hanged for piracy in Canada, a man named Henry Dowsley went to the gallows for piracy in 1865. Dowsley, a Negro, and a white man named James Douglas commandeered the ship *Zero* and killed the captain. Douglas, who had also been sentenced to hang, had his sentence commuted to banishment for life.

April 2, 1809

Murder at Bonne Bay

John Pelley, Joseph Rendale and Richard Cross shared a house at Shallow Cove, Bonne Bay. Although the three had relatives at Rocky Harbour they used the Shallow Cove residence for their fishing and hunting activities.

On April 2, 1809, Richard Cross visited his sister, Sarah Singleton of Rocky Harbour. When leaving, he told her he was going with John Pelley to set traps and would return Friday. Cross did not return as promised. By Sunday there was still no sign of him and his sister became concerned. She sought the help of a neighbour, John Paine, and they searched the shoreline for two days without success. When they came to Shallow Cove they met John Pelley standing in the doorway of his house. Pelley, a suspicious character, was believed to be a fugitive from Irish justice who had murdered his wife.

When asked if he had seen Cross, Pelley replied that he had not. Paine then asked if Rendale was around and Pelley answered, "He's gone off to set traps." Something about Pelley's appearance and conduct alarmed Sarah. Tired from the two days of searching, Sarah and Paine decided to stay the night at Pelley's. Early the following morning they left the house to resume the search. As they walked across a field, Sarah found some cuffs and rackets* belonging to her brother. Connecting these items with Pelley's strange behaviour the day before, Sarah suddenly cried out, "Oh God, my brother has been murdered!" Paine shared Sarah's view and he cautioned her, saying, "Hold your tongue. Pelley is not far away and if he hears you he may come and kill us."

The two returned to Rocky Harbour and enlisted the help of William Morris, William Salmon and Tom Skinner. When they returned to Shallow Cove they found Pelley on a marsh about half a mile from his home. Stories about the incident handed down from generation to generation in the Bonne Bay area suggest that the group forced a confession out of Pelley by forcing his body near a huge fire they had started. Some local writers have made the same claims, but the actual account of Pelley's confession as contained in the Colonial Secretary's Letter Books at the Provincial Archives is as follows.

The group arrested Pelley and returned him to Bonne Bay where they kept him in confinement at a local residence. The following morning as Paine sat near the prisoner drinking tea, Pelley stared strangely at him and began to speak. He said, "Ah, John, I have murdered them both, and you may kill me if you please." Paine asked, "Why in God's name did you kill Cross? He never done you any harm."

Pelley replied, "I would not have harmed a hair on his head. I am very sorry about it all. It started when Rendale told me to go out and cut some wood. I grumbled about it and

---

* Wool mitts and snowshoes.

said, 'If you don't keep quiet I'll knock your liver out.' He came at me and I killed him."

While the Colonial Secretary's records are not complete in regards to the Pelley murder case, records held by the Newfoundland Historical society indicate that Pelley used an axe to murder Cross and Rendale. These records report that after Pelley delivered a blow to Rendale, Cross pleaded, "You wouldn't kill a man would you." Pelley didn't answer. He struck Cross several times with the axe killing him instantly.

When Pelley finished confessing his deed he offered to take Paine to the place where he buried the bodies. A posse of men got together and went with Pelley to the shoreline at Shallow Cove where they found the bodies buried beneath sand and grass.

Pelley appeared before Chief Justice Thomas Tremblett of the Court of Assizes in St. John's on September 1,1809. Following a brief trial he was found guilty of both murders and sentenced by Tremblett to be hanged.

The people of St. John's witnessed the morbid procession of the condemned man followed by the executioner and clergy. On the day of the execution he was tied to a horse-drawn cart which paraded him around St. John's. The display of the condemned man in this way was meant to be a deterrent to others contemplating violent crimes.

The execution procession around town ended at Fort Townshend, where a gallows had been erected. Pelley was escorted up the steps of the gallows and the masked executioner placed a white hood over his head. The crowds gathered closer as the executioner dropped the noose over the head of Pelley, who visibly trembled. The executioner then stepped back to release the trap door. The noose tightened quickly around Pelley's neck and he dropped to an instant death. To die instantly at the hands of an executioner was considered a blessing. Many executions were bungled, causing a lingering death for the condemned man.

March 29, 1826

The Duel

A kick in the rear led to a tragic duel between an army ensign and a senior officer in a small St. John's meadow now known as Robinson's Hill.

Captain Mark Rudkin, a twenty-two-year veteran of the Royal Newfoundland Veteran company, was a respected, dignified and honourable military man. How he felt about the undignified attack is summed up in his own words, "I blush to acknowledge that I suffered this vile indignity. Of all the personal insults one man can give another, a kick is the most galling and degrading."

The dispute surfaced at a party given by a fellow officer on March 29, 1826. There was plenty of rum, and the men played cards for money. Late in the night, when one of the guests, Lieutenant Stanley, noticed the host was tired, he suggested they call it a night. An ensign named Philpot became angry and said, "There is the door. Be off. You have no business to disturb us." Stanley replied, "I can go home if I please sir, without consulting you."

Others in the room suggested that Philpot apologize for his remarks. When he refused, several officers left in protest. As they did, Philpot commented, "That nincompoop. I would as soon have shot at him as not."

Mark Rudkin remained calm and continued playing

Lammy. When the game was tied, the dealer took the pot. Rudkin tied the game and tried to claim the money, but Philpot argued that it should be split. The host agreed with Rudkin.

Philpot threw a pitcher of water into Mark Rudkin's face, twisted him around and gave him a swift kick in the rear. Next day Philpot refused to make an apology and Rudkin challenged him to a duel. Rudkin had no intention of shooting to kill his opponent. He felt if he got off the first shot, Philpot would apologize. But Philpot wanted to kill Rudkin.

The duel was fought at Robinson's Hill. The duelling area was measured at fifteen paces, compared to the normal eight paces used in England. At the first try, both men fired the same time but nobody was hit. Philpot was again asked to apologize but refused and a second round took place. This time, Philpot was hit and died on the spot. Rudkin gave himself up for arrest and, along with his two seconds, was charged with murder.

In his defence, Rudkin told the court, "A blow is certainly a very gross provocation; but, the man who strikes you treats you as if you were upon the level of himself in the scale of creation. But, gentlemen, in a kick, contempt is coupled with violence. It leaves a stain upon the character of the injured party, especially in military life, which verbal apologies can never efface. Had I submitted to this degrading indignity without resenting it as an officer and a gentlemen I would have been branded a poltroon and coward." He explained that he deliberately tried to miss Philpot in the first shot, but that Philpot was trying to shoot him. He added that in the second try he had to aim at his opponent or be shot himself.

Claiming his action was justified, Rudkin told the court that this was the first duel in Newfoundland, but there had been a tragic duel at Halifax. He said the survivor of that duel was acquitted. He also referred to several cases in England where the defendants had been acquitted.

When the jury announced its verdict to the court, it was followed by an uproar. The jury found the defendants guilty, but found no malicious intention on their part. An angry judge told the jury their verdict was not acceptable. He said if they felt no malice existed, they would have either to bring in a verdict of manslaughter or acquit the men altogether. The defence noted that without malicious intent there could be no guilty verdict.

The jury took twenty minutes to arrive at its 'not guilty' verdict. A crowd of friends of the accused men carried them on their shoulders back to the Fort on Lemarchant Road for celebration.

October, 1828

Mutiny-Murder Near St. Pierre

In October 1828 the *Fulwood* set sail from Canada heading for England to purchase provisions. As was the custom in those days, the ship carried a full load of Spanish gold and other coins to make the necessary purchases. When the ship left port, the gold and coin had been locked in several large chests and stored below deck.

Crewmembers did not become aware of the treasure on board until they had been at sea for several days. They banded together, mutinied, stabbed the captain and officers to death and took control of the ship. In their haste to steal the gold the gang overlooked an important consideration. They had no experienced navigator among them.

Between St. Pierre and Miquelon there is a stretch of sand sometimes covered by water known as the Dunes. Many vessels have been shipwrecked at this place. With no one to navigate, the *Fulwood* sailed straight into the Dunes and was wrecked. The ship sank faster than the men could remove all the gold. In desperation they tied together some lifeboat oars to make a raft to carry their gold. The raft broke apart and the chests sank beneath the waves.

Authorities learned of the sinking of the *Fulwood* and went to investigate. They quickly discovered the murder, mutiny and robbery that had taken place. The men were arrested and sent to military authorities in Newfoundland. From there they were taken to London under guard, where they were tried and executed at a public hanging at the Old Bailey Court House.

Many attempts were made to find the gold in the area of the Dunes. During a fishing trip the uncle of Emilienne Parrot of St. Pierre noticed a birch wall protruding from a sandy embankment. He dug at the site and found a quantity of gold. According to Emilienne, her uncle told no one at the time. He took the gold to the Canadian mainland, changed it to French money and returned to St. Pierre, where he built himself an expensive home and furnished it lavishly. Emilienne has two of her uncle's paintings in her home, paintings purchased with the *Fulwood*'s gold.

July, 1833

Butchered at Harbour Grace

The judge and jury must have been in a state of confusion

after listening to the testimony of the two Harbour Grace Irishmen who seemed to be trying to outdo each other in lying to the Court. The two scoundrels, Paddy Malone and Peter Downing, tried to lay the blame on each other for three brutal slayings at Harbour Grace. The two gave a comical dimension to a very tragic story that began a few days after the town of Harbour Grace was almost destroyed by fire in 1832.

Paddy and Peter were employed on a farm owned by Tom Bray. Bray, to protect his fortune during the Harbour Grace fire, buried it in his field. When the fire threat ended he enlisted the help of Paddy Malone to help carry several bags of money back into his house where it was stored in the master bedroom.

Later Paddy and Peter gave conflicting accounts of what happened. Peter Downing claimed Paddy had spawned several plans to steal the money. He said, "Paddy was like the devil himself in tempting me. But I am only a robber, not a killer."

When Peter suggested Paddy involve his two brothers in the plan to avoid having to kill anyone, Paddy refused, claiming they couldn't be trusted. Peter replied, "Well then never mention it again to me, because it is a thing that can't be done by two men without murder, and that is one thing I would never do."

Two months passed before the matter was again discussed by the duo. Paddy commented, "We are two cowards Peter. It is as easy to have the money as it is to walk out the door." Taking a sip of rum, Peter answered, "Ah Patrick, it would be a very good thing but ya know it would not be done without murder. I wouldn't wish all the money in the world if it meant killing those foine people. But...if it could be done without killing I would take part."

Another two months passed and once more the robbery was discussed. Paddy stated, "Ya know, I'd have no scruples at all about killing people of their religion. It is not as if they are Catholic like ourselves. Sure, in the old country we'd have no more scruples to kill one of their preachers more than we would a mad dog."

Peter Downing claimed this had upset him. He commented, "It is the devil speaking through Paddy Malone's mouth. It's not that way here. For glorys sake, they are as charitable and God fearing as any of us."

A month later the two men were again plotting to rob the Brays. This time they agreed that it was necessary to kill the family and maid. That night they hid in the bushes waiting for the house to darken when the family retired for the night. They shared a brew while waiting and argued over who would kill whom. Peter, becoming a little self-righteous, asserted, "It is the devil that is tempting us. I will not do it. Don't you ever mention it to me again." They both blessed themselves, shook hands and left.

Another month passed and Paddy told Peter he had enlisted the help of the maid by offering to marry her. Peter, shocked by this news shouted, "Bejesus, Paddy, my good man, ya can't marry that girl, you got a wife in Ireland." Paddy replied he would work it all out once they got the money.

This latest plan included the murder of Bray, his wife and child. Paddy said he would chop down several doors and crawl out to the street shouting, "a thousand murders." "When the people come I will say some men broke in and robbed us and the maid will pretend she fainted." Paddy added, "Me only concern is that I promised to marry the tart."

According to Peter, he held his ground on refusing to murder the Brays. He left the scene saying, "Never mention it to me again." But Paddy stopped him and offered to kill the Brays if he would kill the maid and the child. Peter agreed. They met Bray in the kitchen. When he turned his back, Paddy, lifting the tomahawk above his head, said to Bray, "It's too good to us you are, soir!" and he let drive with a vicious chopping motion which caught Bray in the back of the neck. A second chop caused Bray to fall dead to the floor.

Paddy then went to the maid's room. As Peter entered, Paddy struck the girl with the tomahawk and she fell back dead on the bed. Paddy told Peter, "Ya were right, Peter, me poor wife would never understand about the girl." Leaving the room, Paddy noticed the child sleeping in its bed and he struck and killed the child with the same tomahawk.

The two searched the house inch by inch but could not find the money. They gathered some jewellery and other items and set fire to the house to cover up the murder. Paddy refused Peter's request to share a drink of Bray's liquor. He warned, "Not a taste. Sure if we did, we might take a drop too much and tell everything." They hid the stolen goods at Bear's Beach and when returning to the town heard the fire bells. They ran towards the flaming shouting, "Whose house is on fire?" When someone answered, "It's the Bray's," Paddy cried, "Bejesus, me clothes are in there.'

When Downing finished his story, Judge Bolton turned to Malone and asked him if he agreed with it. "Yer honour," said Paddy, "Not ten words of truth are in the whole story, soir." He then told his version which was similar throughout to Peter's but placed the full blame on Peter. When he finished Peter shouted, "Every damn word of it is false, yer honour."

Soon after the arrest of the two men, Harbour Grace Magistrate Dr.Stirling had elicted a written confession from Paddy Malone, suggesting it could save him from execution.

Judge Bolton refused to admit this statement to the court, since Dr. Stirling had told Paddy it could save his life. However, he noted that without it the court could not arrive at the truth. He stated, "I believe the confessions of the two culprits were fully much of the same tenor and character, only that each charged the other with being the actual murderer. They differed only as to which one did the bloody deed."

He added, "The murders might have gone undetected if it was not for Edward Pyn and Thomas Kitchen, who entered the burning house in an effort to rescue the occupants. They found Bray face down on the floor and blood running from his head and immediately suspected that someone had killed him."

In less than an hour the jury returned its guilty verdict. To the dismay of the general public, Peter Downing was sentenced to be hanged and gibbeted while the rascal Paddy Malone was given life in prison. Judge Bolton justified this saying, "His life may be spared. He will never again be allowed to infest society with his presence."

Meanwhile, a beam and scaffold had been erected outside the sessions room of the old courthouse. Downing walked confidently to the gallows stopping only to thank a Mr. and Mrs. Purchard for their kindness to him while in prison. His last words before dropping through the trap door were; "I forgive all my enemies. I die in peace with all mankind. May the Almighty God receive my soul."

Following the court's instructions the body was cut down and brought to Harbour Grace. It was transported from St. John's to Portugal cove by stage coach and sent by boat to Harbour Grace where it was gibbeted.

Sometime during the night, people unknown managed to break the chains holding the decomposed body, and drag the remains to the doorstep of Dr. Stirling's house.

When the doctor discovered the awful sight around five a.m. there was a note attached to it which read, "Doctor, doctor, test your skill, for I am Downing of Gibbet Hill. This is your man and you were the cause of bringing him here. Take and bury him or look out should you be the cause of allowing him to be put up again, we will mark you for it. Do your duty and put him out of sight. Truly a friend in Carbonear."

The body was placed in a coffin and buried in the courthouse yard at Harbour Grace.

August 31, 1833

Catherine Snow

The disappearance of a fisherman at Port de Grave led to the hangings of three people from the court house window in St. John's. The tragic affair began when John Snow failed to return home on the night of August 31, 1833. Rumours quickly spread that he had committed suicide—or worse, been murdered. When these stories reached Magistrate Robert Pinsent, he initiated an immediate investigation. The results intensified the mystery over Snow's disappearance.

Police visited Snow's wharf where he was reportedly last seen and discovered evidence of a struggle. The fish were strewn all over the wharf, rinds and trap lines were disturbed and dried blood spattered around the wharf.

Catherine Snow told police that John had left after supper that evening, very angry. She recalled that they had an argument over two of the Snow daughters going to a wake about a mile down the road. John insisted that Mrs. Snow get them back. He grabbed his gun and went outside where he fired it into the air several times. Catherine said she became frightened and took the youngest child to stay with her brother-in-law, Ed Snow, for the night.

She became alarmed next morning when she returned home and there was no sign of John. She sought the help of relatives and friends in searching for her husband. The searchers included Tobias Mandeville, Snow's part-time bookkeeper, and Arthur Springer, Catherine Snow's cousin who worked as a labourer for Snow. Meanwhile, police learned that Snow had not treated the two employees well. This, combined with knowledge of an affair between Springer and catherine Snow, caused them to suspect the two men. Both Mandeville and Springer were arrested.

Catherine Snow, irritated over the arrest, begged the judge to release them to help her harvest the hay and crops because she feared she would lose everything. The Magistrate refused and suggested she hire some help to do the work.

Mandeville had arranged bail, but the friend who put up the bail became concerned that the accused would escape. He withdrew the bail and Mandeville was thrown back into prison. A witness later told the Court that Mrs. Snow had tried to get word to Springer and Mandeville to speak only Irish in jail so the police would not understand them.

To uncover the truth about Snow's disappearance, Magistrate Pinsent arranged for Mandeville and Springer to be locked up in separate cells at his office, separated only by a plank partition. A man was assigned to hide beneath the Magistrate's desk and eavesdrop on any conversation the two suspects might have.

However, Springer spotted the man and shouted, "There's a man under the table." The police officer quickly left the room but his presence had spooked Springer and he asked to meet with the Magistrate. He confessed to participating in the murder of John Snow with Mandeville and Catherine Snow.

The plan was to shoot Snow when he returned that night from his weekly trip to Bareneed. Mrs. Snow assisted by sending her housekeeper and two oldest daughters to a wake about a mile away to ensure that no witnesses would be present. After Snow was killed, Catherine instructed the two men to disrupt the wharf area so it would appear a struggle had taken place.

Catherine Snow was arrested as she attempted to leave the area. She was taken to prison in St. John's and charged along with Mandeville and Springer of murdering her husband. She denied any knowledge of the conspiracy to kill John Snow. She told police that on the day Snow disappeared, Springer had taken a loaded gun to go shoot some dogs which had been a nuisance in the area. She stated, "I heard some gunshots and Springer came back with Mandeville, but he did not have the gun. I asked where the master was and Springer said 'He'll be here soon.' But he didn't come home."

Mrs. Snow insisted she knew nothing of the murder plot and told police that Springer, after learning the Magistrate had visited her threatened to kill her if she told of the animosity that existed between himself and her husband.

The murder trial got underway on Friday January 10, 1834. The Attorney General told the Court that, "Arthur Springers and Catherine Snow's offence was in a degree technically distinguished from Mandeville's. His was simply murder. But owing to the relationship of wife and servant in which the woman and Springer stood towards the murdered party, their crime if proven against them would constitute a murder denominate 'petit treason'."

He added: "The case is the most deeply atrocious and appalling that I have ever seen." He said he intended to show the Court that "an illicit relationship existed between Springer and Mrs. Snow; that they got rid of John Snow to get him out of the way; that they found Mandeville a willing partner and that several of their plans to kill Snow were bungled."

The Attorney-General then outlined the murder plan. He said, "Mandeville was to leave Snow securing the boat and Springer would shoot him as he stepped onto the wharf. The two would then get rid of the body in the open sea. I can't prove which one fired the gun but they were both present for the murder. As to Catherine Snow, there is no direct or positive evidence of her guilt. But I have a chain of circumstantial evidence to show her guilt." He noted among other things that she had kept Springer in her house for two nights after the murder.

Before the trial ended, Springer tried to clear Catherine Snow. He said the statement he had made when arrested, implicating her in a plot, was not true.

In his summation to the jury the judge noted, "The evidence is conclusive against Mandevelle and Springer. But I ask you to pay close attention to the circumstantial evidence against Catherine Snow. If you do not consider it conclusive, then, give her the benefit of the doubt. There is no choice of manslaughter; either you bring in a conviction or an acquittal." In thirty minutes the jury was back with a guilty verdict against all three defendants.

Just three days after the trial began, the execution order of the court was carried out and Mandeville and Springer were hanged. Catherine Snow, who was pregnant, was allowed to give birth to her child and on Monday, July 21, 1834 she was hanged from the window of the old court house in St. John's.

Speculation over the years that Catherine Snow was innocent is based on the Judge's comments to the jury: "You will observe that nothing said by any of the prisoners can be admitted to implicate her in the act. However, her affair of passion with her very much younger cousin was enough to condemn her."

There was a strong belief in her innocence and the Catholic clergy organized a petition to prevent the execution. With the hangman's rope around her neck and standing on the threshold of eternity Catherine's last words were, "I was a wretched woman but as innocent of any participation in the crime of murder as an unborn child."

Although the custom of the Catholic Church at the time was to disallow an executed murderer from being buried in consecrated grounds, Bishop Fleming, as a mark of his belief in her innocence, gave permission for her burial in the Roman Catholic Cemetery on Long's Hill, St. John's.

Records show nothing of what happened to the child born to Catherine in prison. However, in 1987 I received a letter from a resident of Brooklyn, New York who had read my book *Ten steps To the Gallows* which gives a lengthier more detailed account of the Catherine Snow story. He informed me that Catherine's child had later moved to the United States and he was descendent of that child. Reading the story in *Ten Steps to The Gallows* renewed his interest in his family history.

May 19, 1835
Bigotry Leads to Crime

Henry Winton, editor of the *Patriot*, a St. John's newspaper during the early nineteenth century, was the victim of a barbarous criminal act which is among the unsolved crimes of Newfoundland. On Tuesday, May 19, 1835, Winton set out from Carbonear to visit nearby Harbour Grace. He was accompanied by Captain Churchward of the Brig *Hazard*. Winton was travelling on horse back while his friend followed along on foot.

The two were having a pleasant journey but as they approached Saddle Hill the terror began for Henry Winton. Without any warning, a gang of five men disguised with painted faces, rushed from the woods and attacked Winton. The leader ran directly to the newspaperman and delivered a heavy blow to the side of his head with a stone. Winton fell from his horse, bleeding and almost unconscious. But his ordeal was just starting. Two of the attackers seized Churchward, who tried to pull a gun from his belt to defend himself. With Churchward restrained, the others viciously attacked Winton. When Churchward shouted protests he was dragged to the side of the road and his life threatened.

After beating Winton senseless the attackers filled his ears with mud and gravel. When Winton pleaded, "Do you intend to murder me?", an attacker answered, "Hold your tongue, you bastard." He then opened a clasped knife and ordered the others to hold Winton's hands. The victim shut his eyes and, suspecting he was about to be murdered, whispered a silent prayer. The man with the knife seized Winton's right ear and sliced it from his head.

Winton's agonizing screams and Churchward's pleas had no effect on the attackers, who then twisted Winton's head and sliced off his other ear. Winton passed out. When he came to his vision was blurred from the blood that had poured down over his eyes. The attackers had released the Captain unharmed and he rushed to aid his friend, who seemed to be bleeding to death. With blood streaming behind them, the two made their way a distance of a mile and a half to Dr. Stirling's house at Harbour Grace. Dr. Stirling wasted no time in providing emergency assistance to Winton. He stopped the bleeding, bandaged the wounds and allowed Winton time to rest and regain his strength before returning home to St. John's.

News of the brutal and merciless attack on Winton evoked a strong reaction in St. John's. The *Public Ledger* published an article directed to Winton which stated,

> The long meditated deed of blood has been committed. You, the unflinching advocate of civil and religious liberty, have become the victim of frightful ignorance and intolerance. You have survived the wounds inflicted on you by your ruthless butcher. Yours are the scars of honour on which every man will look with admiration. They will be regarded as marks of honour and patriotism, scarcely inferior to those of the hardy veterans who bled and conquered on the field of Waterloo.

Friends of Winton contributed eight hundred pounds sterling to a reward fund and the Newfoundland Government added another five hundred pounds for any information leading to the arrest of the perpetrators of the attack. Some felt that the attackers were members of the predominantly Catholic 'Constitutional Society.' One letter published in a local newspaper signed 'Q' speculated on this possibility. 'Q' wrote that a prominent citizen, using the code name

"Merchant of Venice" had addressed a special meeting of the society held after the attack was made public.

He stated, "I penetrated into this sanctum sanctoriou, their holy of holies; perhaps at some personal risk." The 'Merchant of Venice' is then reported to have said, "I wonder, boys, is there any spy here now. If there is a spy shaking away in a corner to take notes now, let him take care of himself or else we will set our mark upon him."

'Q' concluded his letter by stating, "It is my intention to attend the next meeting, and should anything good transpire, I should perhaps trouble you with a few notes. If I escape safe and sound from the den." Although there was a large reward offered, and police carried out a thorough investigation of the incident, Winton's attackers were never identified. It was believed that religious bigotry motivated the crime against Winton. Some Catholics on the Island felt that Winton's paper was an anti-Catholic publication.

While researching his story I interviewed two descendants of the men who attacked Winton. One man named Power confessed to his family and soon after the attack they moved to the St. John's area. The other man was a Yetman. His descendants also moved to the St. John's area.

Yetman had been born into a family divided by religious strife. At the time his parents were married, his father, an Anglican, and his mother, a Catholic, made an agreement in the presence of a priest that all children resulting from the marriage would be baptized Catholics. However, when Yetman was born the father insisted he be baptized Anglican. The wife pleaded with her husband to honour his agreement and when he refused she grabbed the baby and ran to a nearby wharf. She told her husband that unless he agreed to the baby becoming a Catholic she would jump with the baby into the ocean. The husband gave in and the child was baptized into the Catholic faith. It was this child who, as an adult, led the attack on Winton.

January 12, 1835

Highway Man Hanged

John Flood, a romantic type local highwayman was hanged at the old court house in St. John's on January 12, 1835. Flood was found guilty of robbery and assault. He had held up the stagecoach which travelled between St. John's and Portugal Cove. Passenger ships to communities in Conception Bay operated from Portugal Cove at the time.

John Flood was the last person to be hanged in public in Newfoundland.

Chapter Three

Later Nineteenth Century

June, 1856
The Commerskie Mass Killings

Ranking second only to the mass murder of 99 people in the arson at the K of C Hostel at St. John's in 1942, is the mass killing on the S.S. *Commerskie* at Burin during the mid-nineteenth century.

The Commerskie killings might have gone undetected had it not been for a St. Mary's Bay diver, David Dobbin. Dobbin was well-known throughout Newfoundland for his heroic underwater salvaging of wrecks all along the coast of Newfoundland.

When Dobbin learned that a ship called the S.S. *Commerskie* had gone to the bottom at a place called Silver Cove near Burin, he set out to inspect the wreck with a view to salvaging anything of value left on board. The deep sea diving suit had just been invented and Dobbin was pioneering its use in Atlantic waters. The *Commerskie* carried eighty-four people from Holland, including the captain, crew and members of a wealthy colonization company going to settle in the western

United States. They chartered the *Commerskie* and turned over all their jewellery and wealth to the captain for safekeeping.

The leader of the group was a prominent person and the wealthiest in the group. Records of the event state that "...he was somewhat crude and irascible in his manner, but a good man at that. His wife, who was with him, was a gentle and cultured lady who had been forced by her parents to marry him much against her will."

The captain, a young, charming and handsome man, learned of this at the beginning of the voyage, and cultivated the young lady's affection. Although his own wife was accompanying him on the trip, he promised the girl that he would do away with his wife and her husband to pave the way for them to marry. He developed a plan to kill everyone on board and steal the fortune that they trusted to him for safe keeping. He recruited six crew members for his plan, with the promise to make them rich for life.

His diabolical scheme was simple. They would sink the ship with all on board and take the wealth with them in a lifeboat. The captain chose the deep waters near Burin as the site for the killings, since the area had a history of shipwrecks. The deed would leave no suspicions. He did not consider, and might not even have been aware, that a recent invention — the diving suit — made it possible for a man to go deep into water and remain there for hours.

At the designated time in the dead of night, the conspirators met on deck and readied the lifeboat for departure. The passengers and those crew members who refused to cooperate were all nailed in cabins below deck and the course of the ship steered towards the rocky shoals at Silver Cove.

Four crew members and the captains's wife managed to get on deck. With time running out, and the likelihood that bringing them back to the cabins would result in being rushed by the others, the captain ordered that they be tied to the passenger rails. The killers then left the ship with their stolen wealth and rowed to safety. They reached safety at Burin and reported the loss of their ship with seventy-six people on board. Their story was accepted and the people of Burin showed them a great deal of sympathy. They were taken to St. John's, where they booked passage to England. They left Newfoundland confident they had committed the perfect crime.

Meanwhile, back at Burin, rumours of foul play were circulating. People were wondering why the survivors had so much money in their possession, why no bodies had washed ashore, and if the young lady with the captain really was his wife as he proclaimed. In the midst of these rumours, David Dobbin arrived at Burin with his diver's suit. He paid little attention to the local gossip and set off to carry out his salvage work on the Commerskie.

The first indication that something was wrong was when Dobbin, making his way along the deck of the sunken vessel in his diving suit, felt something strike against his helmet. It was the body of a woman about 24 years old, wearing a blue jacket, red shirt and cloth boots. Her loose brown hair floated around her. He traced the rope tied around her waist to the life rail and cut it loose, allowing the body to float to the surface. He found four crewmen tied in the same fashion and cut them free also.

He then went below deck to check the cabins. He had to force the doors open because they had been nailed shut. When he entered he viewed the harrowing and ghastly sight of seventy-one partly nude men and women lying dead on the floor. Some had huddled in a corner, face down on the floor. Others were half-propped up by an abutment or shelf.

Dobbin removed the victims from the ship and they were buried near Burin in a place called the Plantation. In recovering the bodies, Dobbin found fifty pieces of gold weighing five pounds, amongst a lot of pig iron. He reported the grisly discovery to authorities and a full report was sent to London. Police there tracked down all the killers and they were arrested and tried for the mass killings.

Before Dobbin died, he related the story to Newfoundland historian P.K. Devine. Dobbin said that the captain had been found guilty and hanged from the gallows, probably at Newgate, and the others were given jail sentences. He explained that the others were not executed because they had claimed they were coerced into the plot by the captain, who threatened to kill them if they refused to participate. Another version of the incident in the files of the Newfoundland Historical Society claims that only the girl was spared execution.

May 2, 1861

Politician Murdered

There was a time in Newfoundland history when it took a great deal of courage to enter the political arena, or even to accept a post as an election day official. The General election of 1861 was one such election. Intimidation was rampant; there were beatings, shootings, destruction of property and riots. In Harbour Main on polling day, May 2, George Furey, cousin of the Government party candidate Charles Furey, was shot and killed. The Returning Officer was so intimidated by threats of violence that when the vote count was completed he refused to make the results known. His fear wasn't alleviated by the presence of fifty members of the Royal Newfoundland Regiment sent to the district to keep the peace on election day.

The outcome of the election was left to the House of Assembly to announce. The count in this dual riding was Nowlan-325; Byrne 322; Hogsett, 316; Furey, 310. Hogsett, a lawyer and former Attorney-General, insisted on taking a seat in the Legislature even though he had lost and the outcome of the election had not been properly proclaimed. The Times, a local newspaper, warned Hogsett that, "A forceable entry may propel the perpetration into quite a different atmosphere to answer for the violence. No outrage, my good Sir! or else. You understand?"

The violence at Harbour Main and Harbour Grace forced the Harbour Grace Standard to suspend publication for several days. When the paper resumed printing, no mention was made of the Furey shooting or other election day violence. Meanwhile, Furey and Hogsett, the losers, went to the Legislature at St. John's and took the Harbour Main seats in the House. Furey left when the Speaker insisted that they had no right to be there, but Hogsett had to be forcefully removed. The successful candidates then took their rightful places in the legislature.

The ladies of St. John's boycotted the legislature because of violence expected to take place at the official opening. A member of the House, Kenneth MacLean, was attacked by a mob as he walked to the House, but he managed to break away and outrun his attackers. Another MHA, P.G. Tessier, was followed by the mob but managed to gain entrance to the House before they could catch up with him.

The crowds then turned their energies to property destruction. They demolished Nowlan and Kitchen's General

Store. Judge Robson's stables were burned and the nearby building of the Theological Institute was burned. The mob also burned to the ground the cottage and outhouses of prominent citizen, Hugh Hoyles. An effort to burn the house of the Anglican Bishop failed.

In response, the Prime Minister ordered out the troops. Reporting on this action, The Times stated, "It is melancholy to record that such was the rebellious disposition and conduct of the mob that neither the presence of the magistrate, accompanied by Lieutenant Colonel Grant, officers and men, nor the utmost and unceasing entreaties of the Roman Catholic clergy, could prevail upon the crowd to retire peaceably to their homes. They kept their ground applying the most insulting language to the Colonel and his troops.

"It was not until they had pelted the soldiers and struck the Colonel that the riot act was read." When the crowds refused to move, the Colonel ordered the troops to open fire. Several people were wounded and Father O'Donnell, a Roman Catholic priest, was shot in the foot. When word of the confrontation reached Bishop Mullock he ordered the Cathedral bells rung to summon all Catholics to the church grounds. The crowds were quick to respond and in no time the church yard was crowded. Bishop Mullock pleaded for common sense to prevail and asked his followers to observe the peace. Bishop Mullock was effective and the crowd dispersed and returned to their homes as the Bishop had requested.

January 15, 1870

Alfreda Pike

Thomas Pike and Alfreda Pike were not related, but they were in love with each other. On Wednesday, January 5th, 1870, the attractive seventeen-year-old Alfreda was visiting her grandmother at Harbour Grace. Her home was in a nearby community then called Mosquito, but later renamed Bristol's Hope. Shortly after 6 p.m. she left Harbour Grace to walk home. Witnesses who last saw her alive recalled that a man was walking with her when she left the town, but no-one was close enough to identify the man.

Early the following morning, a boy named Flannery was proceeding along the road in a wagon and noticed a trail of blood in the snow. It didn't take long for him to discover the body of a young girl lying in a pool of blood a short distance from the road. He wasted no time in rushing to Harbour Grace to notify Constable Furey.

Word of the discovery spread throughout Harbour Grace like wildfire, and by the time police arrived at the murder scene, a large crowd had gathered. An article in the Harbour Grace Standard next day stated, "There indeed was seen the body of a girl—dead—murdered—slaughtered by the hand of some miscreant—a devil incarnate, a monster of blood, reeking his savage butchery on this defenceless victim."

What was not known by the writer and the townspeople at the time was that the sadistic killer was standing there with the crowd that day, expressing his horror over the murder. He was one of the most respected residents of the community and the least likely of all possible murder suspects.

The newspaper article described the condition of the

victim, "There lay the body of that poor girl, with the head almost severed from it by a succession of frightful gashes extending from ear to ear through the throat; many violent wounds in and around the face, chin deeply cut, jaw broken, teeth knocked out, and the back part of her head completely battered."

The horror of the scene obviously touched the writer who wrote, "What mind can grasp the intensity of agony which the poor victim must have undergone—the struggle for life, the cry for mercy, the fearful death wounds, the pool of blood, the melancholy tragedy- a human being mangled and butchered by another human being. Ten thousand times worse than the beast that perishes."

The body of the victim was wrapped and taken to a nearby hospital. Crowds of people visited the hospital, and later that evening, Alfreda Pike's body was identified by her brother. A police investigation followed, but with no success.

The Standard tried to encourage public co-operation in its editorial which stated, "We are sure that the feeling of our people is such that everything will be done to help even in the most trifling way towards its solution; particularly too, when a very solemn, moral and legal obligation rests on every person to communicate to the proper authorities any and every information which may tend, even in the slightest degree, to throw light on the question and towards the detention of the guilty. Any person failing to do this will render themselves liable to heavy punishment, in fact, they will be considered as accessories to the murder for such neglect of their duty, and when it becomes known, as it undoubtedly will, they will be dealt with as such. Therefore, we would advise them to take warning before it is too late."

The warning was in vain. No witness came forward and the murderer continued to live in Harbour Grace for several years. He never gave any hint of the burden of guilt which must have rested on his shoulders. The Coroner's Jury conducted an investigation which concluded with a verdict of "Wilful murder against some person or person unknown."

The real murderer went undetected and for the past century, the stigma of suspected guilt rested on the shoulders of the girl's boyfriend, Thomas Pike. Although there was no evidence connecting him with the deed, townspeople made life so difficult for the boy that one day he left Newfoundland for the United States and never returned.

Over fifty years after the murder, the real killer, with his own record still unblemished and still a man respected by the public, lay on his death bed at Grand Falls. No-one knows just how much he had been burdened with the knowledge and memories of what he had done. However, he was remorseful on his death bed and wanted to ease his conscience with a confession.

The man, ex-Harbour Grace Constable Furey, who had been involved in the actual Pike murder investigation, shocked those close to him by confessing that he was the man who killed and mutilated Alfreda Pike.

This revelation might have gone unrecorded if it had not been for a letter written by an employee of the Harbour Grace Post Office who had read the confession when it came through the post office there in 1925. Mr. J. Crocker was bothered by the fact that the suspicion of guilt still lay on the shoulders of Thomas Pike.

Almost twenty years later Mr. Crocker wrote Joey Smallwood who was then broadcasting a nightly radio show called *The Barrelman*. He stated, "I feel an injustice is being done to the descendants of Thomas Pike. I feel the stigma of supposed guilt for so dastardly a deed may still be on his children and grandchildren."

Smallwood choose not to broadcast the story in consideration of "the peace of mind of those who may possibly have some relationship with the dying confessor." The documents relating to the death bed confession ended up gathering dust in a file at the Historical offices at Colonial Building. While researching the story for the book *Too Many Parties, Too Many Pals* I discovered the letter which had stuck to the back of another document and evaded detection all these years.

The murder of Alfreda Pike, considered one of Newfoundland's oldest unsolved mysteries, is a mystery no longer.

November 20, 1871

A Harbour Grace Double Murder

A hand sticking out of a grave drew police attention to a pit on the Geehan family farm at Harbour Grace. Digging through the manure and clay piled on top of the shallow grave, police didn't take long to uncover the body hidden below. The view that greeted them was repulsive. Dressed in canvas trousers, blue stockings, a cravat and sou'wester was a body covered in dried blood. There were wounds on his right arm and chest. His right ear and the fingers of his right hand were missing. Days earlier, a woman's body had been found on the Spaniard's Bay road, two miles from the Geehan farm.

Patrick Geehan, his wife, her brother Garret Sears and a domestic, Johanna Hamilton lived at the Geehan farm on the southern end of Harbour Grace. Patrick Geehan had a strained relationship with his wife and brother-in-law. Geehan was having an affair with Hamilton and had taken her that year to the Labrador fishery with him.

On November 20, all members of the household were working at various chores when Mrs. Geehan uncovered a partially filled bottle of rum Patrick had hidden in the cellar. She grabbed the bottle and ran to her husband shouting, "I'll make a holy show of you."

The two became entangled in a struggle over possession of the bottle and during the fighting Mrs. Geehan was strangled. Patrick later insisted he had not meant to kill her. He told Johanna to let him know when Sears was returning from the field. He was afraid of Sears, a powerful man with a quick temper. Geehan loaded his rifle and sat in the corner of the kitchen waiting Sears' entry.

When Johanna gave the signal, Geehan raised his rifle. He described to police what then happened: "As soon as the shot was fired, he bawled and called me by name, then wheeled and fell face down and, with the fall, stunned himself. I thought he was dead. I made sure he was dead. I wanted to put him out of his misery. I gave him one blow with the pole end of the hatchet and that's all. I didn't want to mangle or cut him up."

Although Johanna was frightened she reluctantly agreed to help Patrick hide the bodies. They hid the victims beneath hay behind the barn. However, when they returned to move them at two a.m. next day they discovered that the pigs had eaten Sears' right ear and fingers of his right hand.

They laid Mrs. Geehan alongside a road about two miles from the farm. Sears was buried in a shallow grave on the farm which Geehan covered with clay and manure. A neighbour, Daniel Shaugharoo, unsuspectingly stood near Sears' grave next morning as Geehan added clay and manure to hide the body.

For the next three days Geehan told neighbours that his wife and her brother had gone to St. John's so Sears could get medical attention for his sore toe. When Mrs. Geehan's body was found, Geehan told mourners that his wife likely dropped dead while walking the road. He pretended to be puzzled by the fact that Sears did not return for the funeral.

Meanwhile, neighbours were suspicious. Shaugharoo related to others that Geehan had marks on his face which he claimed he received when cutting hay. Others attending Mrs. Geehan's wake noticed marks and bruises on her throat and forehead.

After his wife's funeral, Patrick went to a Brigus tavern where he chatted with Police Constable Tobias Hackett. Hackett was puzzled by the whole affair and the next morning began a search of the Geehan property. He discovered Geehan and Hamilton sleeping in the same room. There were two beds in the room and Geehan explained they slept in the room together because they were lonely. The search also detected bullet holes in the tailboard of Geehan's cart. There were also blood stains on the cart. Neighbours told police that they heard shooting from the Geehan farm on the same day the two victims had disappeared. Geehan and Hamilton were arrested.

Meanwhile, the wind and animals had removed enough clay from the grave of Sears to uncover his hand. The sighting of the hand from the grave lead police to the site. Immediately after learning of the discovery, Geehan told police he had accidentally shot Sears as he tried to shoot a hawk. He said, "Johanna sang out, 'We will be hung, the people will hear him bawling.' She passed me the pitchfork and said, 'Kill him with this,' I did it and killed him."

This story was denied by Johanna. Both Hamilton and Geehan were charged with the murder of Garret Sears.

The trial got underway in Supreme Court at St. John's on May 29, 1872. The defendants were represented by Richard Raftus who was admitted to the bar the day after the trial started. This was his first case.

The Crown presented evidence by Catherine Hearn, a neighbour who testified that Johanna Hamilton had told her that Mrs. Geehan would be dead by Christmas. She recalled, "After the body of Mrs. Geehan was found I got a great shock, and the words Johanna had said came to memory."

Another witness, Patrick Morrissey, gave an uncanny account of his experience a day after Mrs. Geehan's funeral. At the time Sears' body still had not been discovered. Morrissey testified, "I saw this man coming down the road, his face was pale, he looked queer. I got frightened. I said to myself, let Garret Sears be dead or alive that is him. I said this without knowing anything had happened to him." When Morrissey tried to follow Sears down to Geehan's, his wife and children, who had also seen the man, persuaded him to stay away.

Next day, Morrissey asked Geehan if Sears had returned the previous night. Geehan's head dropped and he answered, "Sears didn't go down the road last night unless he went down dead." Geehan then asked Morrissey if he felt Sears could have killed his own sister. Morrissey answered that he never heard of such a thing but he did read of the husband killing the wife or the wife killing the husband. He then said to Geehan, "Farewell, now forever more. I don't know why I said that but I did."

Johanna Hamilton denied participating in the double murder. She told the court that Geehan didn't get along with his wife or with Sears. However, she said,"I never witnessed Geehan strike Sears, but I witnessed Sears strike Geehan." On Monday, June 3, after a two-hour and forty-five minute deliberation, the jury returned its verdict of guilty. Geehan was sentenced to be hanged.

Before going to the gallows, Geehan gave a written statement to Bishop Howley which was to be published after his death. In it, he swore Johanna was not involved in the murders. He stated, "I never up to the time of Garret Sears death said one word to her on such a subject nor did any conversation ever take place between us to that effect."

Johanna Hamilton received a reprieve from hanging because she was pregnant. Unlike Catherine Snow, who was executed in 1834 after giving birth, Hamilton was deported after serving eight years in prison.

Patrick Geehan became the first person to be executed and buried inside Her Majesty's Penitentiary. He was buried in the northwest corner of the prison yard.

December 1, 1874

On December 1, 1874, a young man named Peter Angel was involved in a fight at Petty harbour. the next day his body was found floating in the harbour. A coroner's inquest was held at Petty Harbour and there was evidence of additional violence inflicted upon the victim. No arrests were made in this case and it remains among Newfoundland's unsolved mysteries.

1876

A still unsolved murder took place at Burin in 1876. John Bassett was employed as a sort of wharf supervisor for Messrs. de Quettsville. Bassett was a fair and just man, but he was hot tempered and made many enemies among local fishermen. Several threats were made against his life, but he didn't take them seriously.

Bassett regularly walked in the evening along the road leading to Upper Burgeo. One such evening he left the company of three friends and was not seen alive again. His body was found the next morning floating in the bay. A sou'wester was tied tightly under his chin by a strong line. Bassett had been savagely beaten. His nose, jaws, teeth and arms were broken and his pockets were filled with rocks. A large rock was tied to his wrist in an effort to sink the body. There was also evidence that the victim had been burned. A police investigation failed to solve the crime.

March 9, 1880

The Artist At HMP

Two things stand out in the life of Alexander Pindikowski. The first is that he was a very talented Polish artist. The second was that he was a convict at Her Majesty's Penitentiary at St. John's, Nfld. Unlike other criminals, Pindikowski is remembered not for the crime he committed, but for the beautiful art work he left behind.

The artist's Newfoundland criminal experience started after his arrival here in 1879. The Anglo-American Telegraph Company operated a cable office at Heart's Content. The company was civic minded and treated its employees and the community very well. It was the Telegraph company's effort to help its employees that resulted in Pindikowski coming to Newfoundland in the first place.

The company hired the Polish artist to give art instruction to interested members of its staff at Heart's Content. He enjoyed instant popularity among the residents of the community. During 1873 the old Anglo-American Telegraph office, which had been constructed in 1867, was converted into a theatre by the company. Pindikowski was commissioned to paint six twenty-five-foot-long backdrops for the stage.

Things went well for the Pole.He was doing work he liked. He made many new friends and he was admired and respected by all. Then his luck began to change.

Early in 1880, Pindikowski found himself in St. John's and short of money. He thought to solve his problem by forging a cheque in the name of Ezra Weedon, Esquire, chief of the Anglo-American Telegraph Company's staff at Heart's Content. The artist took the cheque to the commercial bank and handed it to a teller named Cooke. The cheque was made out for two hundred and thirty two pounds, which in those days was a considerable sum. For some reason, Cooke became suspicious and refused to cash the cheque. Pindikowski returned a second time, but with a lesser amount. He now submitted a cheque for sixty-five pounds. This time Cooke wired Mr. Weedon enquiring about the cheque and received a quick reply stating that Weedon had not issued any cheques to Pindikowski. Cooke contacted Inspector Carty and reported the incident.

Inspector Carty, accompanied by Sergeant Sullivan, began a search of the city to locate the artist. In those days, the Total Abstinence Society of St. John's operated a coffee house in the downtown area. At this house, non-alcoholic refreshments were served during and after business hours. Recreational activities were available and the house had a reading room for patrons. It was at this coffee house that the search ended. On the night of March 9th, 1880, the police arrested the Polish artist and escorted him to the lock-up. He was charged with attempting to pass a forged cheque. On June 8th, he was sentenced to fifteen months' hard labour at HMP. Included in the sentencing was an order that he leave Newfoundland within five days after his release; and if he ever returned, he would be jailed again for two years.

Pindikowski was then escorted to HMP to start serving his time. However, his reputation as an artist and fresco painter resulted in his getting the opportunity to do work on the 'outside'. He was assigned to paint and decorate the ceilings in the state rooms of government House. His work so delighted Governor Glover that he suggested to Prime Minister Whiteway that the artist be assigned to decorate the ceilings of the two legislative chambers in the Colonial Building. This job was followed by the paintings of the ceilings at Presentation Convent.

The artistic work of Alexander Pindikowski earned him five weeks remission from his sentence and gained him many supporters and friends in St. John's. These friends collected an amount of money equal to the amount forged and succeeded in having him released from prison. For a short while after his release, he set up a business in the city. The business was a failure and Pindikowski left Newfoundland never to return, but his work in St. John's continues to draw much praise.

October 8, 1883
Escape From HMP

One of the most successful escapes from Her Majesty's Penitentiary in St. John's was carried out by a Horse Cove fisherman named Michael Whelan. At the time of the escape, Whelan had served four years of a life sentence for the murder of Levi King.

The incident which resulted in King's death and Whelan's imprisonment started on Saturday afternoon, October 8th, 1883. Whelan had stopped at a beer shop located at the foot of Kenna's Hill for a few drinks of spruce beer and rum. While there, he met George Squires, a neighbour. The two sat and drank for almost an hour. Squires had just returned from the fishery and was anxious to get home to his family. When Whelan and his wife got up to leave, Squires asked for a ride with them to St. Phillips.

The trio boarded the horse-drawn carriage and headed up Portugal Cove Road towards St. Phillips. Squires later told the police, " At that time, Whelan was rowing and jawing with me all the time. But he didn't touch me. I got off his cart at Kenny's Farm and walked ahead. But he overtook me and passed me on Lawlor's Hill."

Squires said that when Whelan challenged him to a fight, he ran ahead and jumped on a cart driven by Henry Jones. When Whelan followed behind shouting insults, Squires jumped from the cart to seek protection on another cart driven by Richard Tucker and Levi King.

In a matter of minutes, the two carts were racing in over the Cove Road with Whelan gaining the lead and finally forcing Tucker to bring his horse to a halt. Whelan jumped off his cart and asked Squires if he still had a bottle of rum, which he had displayed earlier at the beer shop. Whelan then became verbally abusive towards Squires. The two walked side by side arguing over the rum. When they got to a place known as Brigg's Bridge, Whelan challenged Squires to a fight. Squires prudently refused to tangle with the two-hundred pound, six foot tall Whelan. He ran ahead and again joined Tucker and King.

Whelan got back on his carriage and began cursing the Orange Lodge and all Orangemen. Richard Tucker asked, "Mick, what need you bother about Orangemen?" Whelan answered, "It's what they done to our fathers. They got a lodge built now at the Cross Roads without a window or anything else in it. Why are they so secret?"

Tucker chided Whelan saying, "You're on the wrong side, Mick boy." That was too much for the rowdy Irishman. He jumped from his cart and ran to the side of Tucker's shouting "I'm on the right side now. Get down off that cart and I'll fight you all." Seeing his challenge was going unanswered, Whelan stepped back and roared, "There's not the principle of a man among ya. Get off the cart. Get off and kill me. I'm not afraid to die."

Undaunted by Whelan's threats, Levi King said calmly, "We have better principles than to do the like."

Whelan moved closer to the cart and asked King, "Do you think you can do it? Get off the cart and we'll see," King replied, "I wouldn't want to be able to do it, Mick."

Whelan quipped, "Is there anything you fellows can do?" to which King replied, "Yes, we can haul down yer Chapel." All three aboard King's cart burst out laughing which only added fuel to Whelan's burning temper.

When Whelan attempted to pull King down from the

cart, Tucker whipped the horse and they dashed away, leaving Whelan shouting obscenities and cursing all Orangemen.

The trio arrived at King's house and went inside. Levi King picked up a hatchet helve* and said, "If Whelan comes here he won't bother us." No sooner had the words been spoken than Whelan could be heard outside, challenging anyone and everyone in the house to come outside and fight.

King was the first to out and face Whelan. Tucker, Squires and King's wife followed. After a brief exchange of insults between Whelan and King, Whelan stooped and ran towards King, grasping King's legs and throwing him to the ground. Whelan then pulled a knife and stabbed King in the groin. King got to his feet and attempted to run back to the house, but Whelan stabbed him again in the back.

Whelan then turned and attacked Squires, however, Squires stepped aside and delivered a forceful blow to Whelan's temple driving him head over heels to the ground. Not waiting for the hot tempered Whelan to regain his senses, Squires followed his friends into the King house and locked the door.

As Whelan got back on his feet, his wife grabbed him by the arm and coaxed him aboard the cart. The two then drove off down the road. King, who had been sitting on a kitchen chair, moaned, then keeled over onto the floor. It was only then that the others noticed he had been stabbed. When Squires saw the knife wound in the victim's left groin area, he covered it with a half stick of tobacco.

Squires sent for a doctor and as he moved around to help his dying friend, he noticed that he too had been stabbed. His wound was a minor one. It seemed that during his brief

---

* Handle.

scuffle with Whelan, the knife nicked his left side between the hip and the ribs. By the time the doctor arrived, King was dead. The incident was reported to the police.

Constable Alfred Rees led two other constables to Whelan's home to make the arrest. Whelan and his wife locked themselves inside and refused to open the door. Rees tried to persuade Mrs. Whelan to allow them in, but she held firm in support of her husband. Finally, the police forced entry into the house.

On October 6th 1883, Michael Whelan was brought before Justices Carter, Pinsent and Little, and charged with the wilful murder of Levi King. The trial lasted one day and the jury took only one hour to reach its verdict. The jury reduced the charge and found Whelan guilty of manslaughter. They did not recommend mercy and Whelan was sentenced to life imprisonment.

Four years later, Whelan's good behaviour had earned him the trust of the prison officials. On the morning of November 25,1887 he was permitted outside prison walls to work with other trusted prisoners on a drainage system they were constructing for the General Hospital.

A fight broke out amongst the prisoners and when the guards moved in to break it up, Whelan seized the chance to make his dash for liberty. He ran down alongside Quidi Vidi Lake with a prison guard in close pursuit. He outdistanced the guard and soon disappeared into the White Hills.

McCowan, a superintendent of the prison, ordered a search for the fugitive and a two-hundred dollar reward was offered by the colonial secretary's office for Whelan's recapture. He was never recaptured. Many thought he had drowned while trying to swim across the Harbour. Others suspected he escaped and was living in the United States. Adding fuel to the claim he had made it to the U.S. was the fact that soon after the escape his wife left Newfoundland and moved to New York.

Whelan's escape remained one of Newfoundland's unsolved mysteries until the mid 1980's when, while researching one of my books on crime, I discovered evidence which verified that Whelan had succeeded in making it to the U.S. His wife joined him and they reared a family there. However, on his death bed he confided to a priest of his past crime and escape from a Newfoundland prison. This revelation was published in New York newspapers in the 1930's. In my research I came across a published account of that confession.

January 1, 1888

Guillotined

During the early morning hours of New Year's Day, 1888, neighbours were alarmed by loud noises coming from Francois Coupard's cabin on Ile Aux Marins, St. Pierre. The next morning they complained to the local police. Two inspectors made a casual investigation. They saw nothing out of the ordinary and concluded that the owner had gone bird-hunting. Later that day two of Coupard's friends entered the house and were sickened by what they discovered. Behind a sail draped across the kitchen was their friend Francois, covered in blood.

Police were summoned again; this time they had the local doctor with them. The body was stretched out on the floor and the terrible mutilation noted in the doctor's records. The chest had been ripped from left to right. His throat had been cut, and there was a knife wound through the heart. The stomach was ripped apart and his intestines were hanging out. A report stated, "Other things were done to the body which were too sickening to mention."

Suspicion immediately fell upon Coupard's boarder, Louis Ollivier and his friend Augustus Neel. Police learned that the two had tried to sail to Newfoundland but were forced back by bad weather. They then set out to walk to St. Pierre. Police caught up with them and took the duo into custody. It didn't take long to get a confession.

Ollivier, twenty-six years old, and Neel, twenty-nine, stated that they were drunk at the time of the killing. They told police they ripped the victim open "...to see if he had any fat." The trial started on February 8, 1889.

Evidence given during the trial showed that the two accused men kicked in the door of Coupard's cabin. The victim met them with a knife in his hand. Ollivier struggled with him and then Augustus joined in the fight. He screamed, "It's better to kill the devil than have the devil kill you." He took the knife from Coupard and plunged it into Coupard's stomach. When Coupard ceased to struggle, the men lit a candle to see if he was still alive. He was still breathing. Neel then began plunging the knife into Coupard's chest until he managed to cut his heart right from his body. Holding the heart, Neel shouted, "What a big heart." He continued to mutilate the body and then placed it in a sitting position behind the canvas sail.

Ollivier told the court that he liked Coupard but because of his drunken state he blindly followed Neel's orders. Others testified that Neel was really drunk but that Louis Ollivier appeared to be sober. In spite of this, the prosecution had more sympathy for Ollivier because it was felt that Neel had a sort of hypnotic hold over Ollivier.

The two were found guilty but only Neel was sentenced to be guillotined. Since there was no guillotine on the islands, the death machine had to be imported. Legend on the islands says the guillotine imported was the one used to kill Marie Antoinette, Robespierre and twenty-one of his loyal followers. French records say the machine was an old one and probably the first one used in France. Dr. Louis, the life-secretary of the Academy of surgeons designed it, and it was constructed by a man named Schmidt. Originally it had been painted a dull blood red.

Jean Marie Legent, a prisoner doing time for theft, was given five hundred francs and his freedom if he and his brother would act as executioners. They agreed. Jean Marie was given a fishing knife in case the guillotine failed. Before being escorted to the execution site, Neel was given a glass of wine and a cup of tea. As he left his cell he commented, "Who would have believed that the land would have me after the sea could have had me hundreds of times?"

Before being executed he addressed the crowd of spectators. He said, "Let my example serve a lesson. I killed and now I am going to be killed. Do not do like me." He then stepped towards the priest and kissed the crucifix. He asked the priest to bring his body to the cemetery as he didn't want to be buried like a dog. Neel placed his head on the block and encouraged the executioner saying, "Come on then, and don't miss me." Jean-Marie released the blade but, to the horror of the crowd, it failed to sever the victim's neck. The executioner then took his knife and finished the job.

Public reaction to the execution was so strong that the Doctor who was to take the body for medical study changed his mind and refused to accept it.

Jean-Marie Legent had two children. He was released from prison and given five hundred francs as promised.

However, when he tried to pay his bills, the local shopkeepers refused to accept what they described as, 'blood money.' Neither would anyone on St. Pierre give him work. Authorities had to step in and arrange transportation to France for Legent and his family. They left St. Pierre on September 17, 1889 aboard a fishing vessel named *LeDrac*.

The place where Neel was executed was renamed 'Place Neel' and it is still known today by that name.

December, 1888
The Scrooge of Water Street

*E*benezer Scrooge and Bob Cratchett of Charles Dickens' *A Christmas Carol* could have been based on the relationship between Archibald Sillars and William Parnell: Sillars, the overbearing, heartless, money-hungry Scrooge and Parnell, the warm-hearted, family loving Cratchett, loved by all. While comparisons can easily be made between the Dickens' characters and the two St. John's men, the outcome of both relationships was quite different.

Scrooge had the help of the three Ghosts of Christmas to change his life and relationship with the Cratchett family, while Sillars' harshness and nagging was stopped only by three bullets and a bloody beating.

Archibald Sillars, the Scrooge of Water Street, had amassed a fortune from his ownership of a general merchandising firm. William Parnell had been employed by Bowring Brothers for twenty years and was looking for a business opportunity. The paths of the two came together in 1888 when Parnell raised sufficient money for a sizeable down payment to purchase the firm from old Sillars, who had decided to retire. Sillars vacated the apartment over the store and moved to Freshwater Road while Parnell, his family and household staff moved into the vacated apartment.

However, Parnell's jubilation over becoming a Water Street merchant came to a swift end when he learned that Sillars had defrauded him. The Scotsman had overvalued the stock in the store and maintained the right to collect money owed to the business for himself. To aggravate matters, Sillars turned many customers away by harassing them to pay outstanding bills while they were visiting Parnell's.

Parnell opened a line of credit with the Bank to keep the business going, but Sillars used his influence to persuade the Bank to refuse Parnell credit. Sillars' actions forced the creditors to take over the business. They set up three trustees, including Sillars, to oversee the business. Parnell was given a fifty dollar monthly salary and household expenses.

After that, Sillars made life even more unbearable for Parnell. He harassed the entire Parnell family and on one occasion struck Parnell's son for taking an apple from the barrel. He even made insulting remarks to Mrs. Parnell.

Like Cratchett, who for the sake of his family tolerated the harshness of Scrooge, Parnell tolerated Sillars. His lawyers, McNeily and McNeily, advised him to put up with Sillars until he repaid the creditors.

On November 30, 1888, a light snowfall signalled the advent of the Christmas season. The advancing season had no effect on the icy heart of Sillars. When the store closed that night Sillars and Parnell met in the basement office of the store. Parnell's children had been sick all week with fever. He had been up all night with them and was very tired. Sillars admonished him about falling asleep on the job. When Sillars complained that the creditors might not get their just dividends, Parnell replied they would get the same as the previous year but he would seek better terms. Sillars shouted, "I am the chief creditor and I will not agree."

"You should be last to object considering all the old truck you pawned off on me at triple its value," retorted Parnell. Sillars was outraged and warned, "At the end of the year I will close you up. You and your family will have to clear out. You can all starve and be damned!"

The argument intensified with Parnell calling Sillars a "swindler and a scoundrel," and Sillars insisting he would not condone Parnell's audacity.

Parnell had a .32 calibre Colt Pistol which he used to protect the store. When Sillars threatened him with a shovel, Parnell pulled the revolver and fired three shots into the Scotsman. Sillars still had life in him. He struggled to crawl to the stairway. The now enraged Parnell grabbed the shovel and beat the wounded man over the head with it until his body lay motionless in a pool of blood.

When Parnell realized what he had done he went to his upstairs apartment, penned a suicide letter to his family, and consumed a mixture of strychnine and brandy.

His wife found him still breathing and sent for help. Two doctors were soon at his side and managed to save him from the poison. Parnell grasped the doctor's hand and said, "I am not the only one. You will never see Sillars again." When the doctor asked if Sillars had gone home, Parnell replied, "He has gone to his long home. He has driven me to this. He robbed me of every cent I had. He was going to put my poor family on the street to starve."

Sillars' body was found at seven a.m. next morning and Parnell was arrested and charged with murder.

The prosecution's case was simple. They argued that the evidence showed Parnell was losing his business and therefore had motive. He was the last person seen in the basement with the victim. The windows and doors were locked so that no outsider could have committed the crime. The Crown's key witness was Dr. A. Harvey, who reluctantly told of Parnell's confession when being revived.

The defence characterized the Scrooge type personality of Sillars and portrayed Parnell as a true gentleman. The Governor of HMP testified that in the six months Parnell was incarcerated while awaiting trial, he was a model prisoner. The defence argued that Parnell was insane.

The judge pointed out to the jury that there was no evidence that a struggle had taken place before the shooting. Parnell was found guilty and sentenced to hang on July 8 from a gallows inside the Penitentiary. His wife spent several hours with him the night before the execution and a minister stayed with him until midnight. He arose at 5:15 a.m. and invited the guard to come into his cell to join him in prayer. He then shook hands with all present and went to meet the executioner.

The executioner was a small-framed man. He wore a grey coat and a grey woolen cap pulled down over his face. He looked peculiar as he stood near the lever wearing no boots, with his pants tucked into stockings above his knee.

As the executioner's hand reached to grip the release lever, Parnell raised his head to heaven and said, "Lord Jesus, receive my soul, Lord Jesus, into Thy hands I commend my spirit."

As the trap door sprung open Parnell's body disappeared into the darkness of the scaffold. The executioner had made the hanging rope too long. Parnell was a heavy man. When he fell through the scaffold his head was severed. He was buried inside the prison. However, in the 1980s his body, along with several others executed inside the prison, was removed and buried in an unmarked grave at the Holy Sepulchre Cemetery on Topsail Road.

July 20th, 1890

Sadistic Inmate Escapes HMP

Residents of the Avalon Peninsula had good reason to be concerned on the night of July 20th, 1890. News had already spread from community to community across the peninsula that the infamous James Rigby had escaped from Her Majesty's Penitentiary in St. John's. Rigby was serving a five year term at the prison for manslaughter and was considered to be a dangerous man.

Rigby's crime took place on board the *Clara* in October, 1888. When the crew went to the galley for lunch after a hard morning's work, Rigby, the cook, ordered the slow, dim-witted Charles Hookey to take his meal on deck and eat alone. While Hookey walked from the galley, Captain Sparkes tripped him, causing him to drop his food and fall to the floor. Rigby and the Captain then began kicking and punching him. Hookey managed to get to his feet and quietly went to the sleeping quarters to avoid his tormentors.

A few days later Rigby and the Captain cornered Hookey on deck and viciously attacked him again. They punched and kicked him and when he fell to the deck, Rigby jumped on his stomach, causing him to black out. The injuries forced Hookey to bed for several days. Rigby refused to feed him and allowed him to have only bread and water. Anytime he attempted to get out of bed, Rigby would kick him back. On one such occasion he knocked Hookey unconscious.

Later, after recovering, Hookey was ordered to steer the ship. When he stumbled on his way to the wheel, Rigby and the Captain beat him until blood flowed from his ears. Once again he was forced to bed. The next day, Hookey was reefing the topsail when he became ill and climbed down. Once on deck Rigby and Captain Sparkes savagely attacked him. They punched him, kicked him, and jumped on his stomach. His ears and nose bled and his face swelled. Other crew members, in terror of Captain Sparkes and Rigby, waited until the two left and then carried the brutalized victim to his sleeping quarters. He was in bed for a week. Although Rigby again ordered that he be given only bread and water, the crew brought him blankets and food. At one point Rigby paid him a visit and shouted, "If we were bound for the United States instead of St. John's you'd be gone for long ago."*

When the Captain walked into the cabin he called Hookey "a fraud." The two aggressors then dragged him from his bed to the deck and strapped him to a pump. They left him there, partially clothed, to face the cold Atlantic winds and rain. Hookey broke free but was too scared to go below deck. A witness described his condition, "His ear was swollen and mortified. It was like a piece of beef. The following day, he did not come on deck. Rigby and the captain dragged him up and made him work. That day he was given only bread and water."

When the vessel was just three days from St. John's, Captain Sparkes began showing concern for Hookey. He gave him medicine and treated him better. The Captain hoped that Hookey would recover before the ship arrived in St. John's. He was concerned the authorities would learn of

---

* Reference to death penalty in Nfld.

his brutality. However, his compassion came too late. Hookey died. Witnesses said that when the body was laid out for burial, "the head, face and body of the deceased were found to be covered with black sores and swollen. His person was very emaciated and his body covered with vermin." The body was buried at sea thirty-five miles from St. John's. To cover the violence against Hookey the Captain changed records in the logbook and forced a crew member to sign them. He then warned the crew that when they went ashore not to mention anything about the incident. However, the tragedy weighed heavily on their minds, and several crewmembers reported the incidents to local authorities.

The Captain and Rigby were arrested and charged with manslaughter. The Attorney General told the court that "Hookey, on the first day of the trip was a sound and healthy man, but after some time on board, he appeared to be rather dull and stupid. From the severe beatings he received from the accused, he became almost senseless. The only provocation was that he was not a good worker."

Meanwhile, the defence was upset because they could not call the defendants to the stand. Under the criminal law of England, which applied to Newfoundland, prisoners in this kind of trial were not allowed to give evidence. The defence lawyer argued, "This is a cruel law and the sooner it is wiped off the statue books, the better for humanity and justice." The jury found both men guilty as charged.

The judge sentenced them to five years each at HMP. Charles Fox Bennett had asked that mercy be shown Captain Sparkes because he had a wife and two infant children to support. Sparkes served a short period in prison and was granted a pardon. He was ordered to leave Newfoundland and never return.

An unusual incident occurred at HMP when Rigby was

serving time. Two friends had promised that after their release they would return to celebrate Christmas with Rigby in his cell. On Christmas Day the two broke into the prison and succeeded in sharing liquor and tobacco with their friend Rigby. They were later captured and sentenced back to HMP. This was likely the only case on record of anyone breaking into HMP.

On July 20, 1890, Rigby used a knife to unscrew the latch to his cell and managed to escape. He passed two guards who were sleeping in the hallway. Both had guns, but the prisoner chose not to steal the weapons.

His escape was short lived. A massive search was started by police. All vessels in the harbour were searched. However, police found the escapee hiding in a wooded area in the Topsail area.

January 19, 1894

Murder on Springdale Street

The Brass Castle was nothing like its name suggests. Actually it was a dilapidated tenement located at the lower end of Springdale Street in downtown St. John's. It was used as a residence and scrap metal business by its owner William McCarthy. It was also the scene of one of Newfoundland's unsolved murder mysteries.

Eighty-year-old Billy McCarthy was well known around St. John's. He was considered a penny-pinching eccentric, and while he lived in apparent squalor, many people believed he had a fortune hidden in the old rundown residence he called home. This belief may have cost him his life.

Even Billy's wife found him a difficult person to get along with. Mrs. McCarthy chose to live in a tidy two-story home at 14 Adelaide Street, where she operated a small grocery store.

At about 10:30 p.m. on the night of January 19th, 1894, Mrs. Jewer, a neighbour, dropped in to pay a visit to Billy McCarthy. She was a little concerned because she hadn't seen him since one o'clock that afternoon. What she viewed when she stepped into the darkened kitchen of McCarthy's home sent her screaming out the front door for help. McCarthy was sprawled across the floor with his head and clothing covered with blood.

Constable Ed Murphy was walking the beat near the Brass Castle that night. Alerted by the screams of the woman running from the house, Murphy, followed by three men who were standing nearby, rushed into McCarthy's kitchen. The policeman lit a lantern, and its irregular glow cast an eerie light across the ghastly scene on the kitchen floor.

There McCarthy lay, dead. He was resting face down and it was apparent that the back of his skull had been bashed in. Blood covered his head and clothing and had spattered most of the furniture in the room.

Murphy searched the house and the area adjoining the kitchen, which McCarthy used for his scrap metal business. On the head of a barrel, he found what sppeared to be the murder weapon. It was a piece of gun pipe about two and a half feet long and stained with blood. Dr. Pike was called to the scene, and after officially declaring old Billy McCarthy dead, arranged for the body to be moved to the City Morgue.

The heavy snow storm that battered the City the next day did not delay the spreading of reports of the murder at the Brass Castle. Friends of the family made their way through the storm to McCarthy's widow's store on Adelaide Street to comfort her and to help with the funeral arrangements. A place was cleared in the parlour and later that day the coffin containing McCarthy's body was delivered to be waked.

Meanwhile, police were at the scene of the murder trying to piece together the mystery. The fact that they found no money, coupled with the widespread belief that McCarthy had a lot of money, led the police to believe the motive for the murder was robbery. They had two suspects. One was an unidentified man who was seen leaving the Brass Castle at 9:30 on the evening the murder occured. The second suspect was a man who sold scrap metal to McCarthy earlier that day.

Peter Carrigan, who worked as a fireman at the old fire station on New Gower Street, met the description of the man seen leaving the murder scene at 9:30 p.m. Carrigan was taken into custody by the police. They gathered his clothing and sent it to a medical examiner, who carried out a microscopic examination of blood stains found on them.

Police believed the victim was murdered at about seven p.m. This was based on the report given police by William Cuddihy, who lived in a boarding house on New Gower Street. He reported that just when he finished supper a little girl came into the house and said, "Old man McCarthy has been killed by the bar of the door falling on him." The little girl said she was told of the old man's death by Mrs. Jewer who lived next door to the Brass Castle. Mrs. Jewer was also taken into custody by police and after thorough questioning, was released.

The police case against Carrigan disintegrated when his fellow workers at the Fire Hall came forward to say that the accused was with them all evening on the day of the murder. For months after, police followed hundreds of leads which led nowhere. In one incident, a policeman's wife went into a store on Water Street just around the corner from the Brass Castle. When the storekeeper passed her a four dollar note as change she noticed there was blood on it. She showed the note to her husband, and an hour later the storekeeper was questioned by police. He explained that the money had rested on a piece of venison at the store and had been stained with blood. He was released.

For decades after people talked about the Brass Castle murder. Often they speculated on who might have killed McCarthy. While old newspaper records mentioned the speculation they did not mention the suspect's name, except to note he was a neighbour of McCarthy, and was never short of money after the killing and robbing of Billy McCarthy at the Brass Castle.

July 14, 1895
Triple Murder at Mundy Pond

The discovery of the bodies of a mother and her two infant children with their throats slit sent shock waves throughout the city of St. John's. Hundreds of men, women and children dropped what they were doing and made their way to the Conroy residence located in Brazil's Field near Mundy Pond. The Evening Telegram described the affair as the most terrible crime in the annals of Newfoundland criminal history.

This tragedy began to unfold on the morning of July 14, 1895 when John Conroy and his wife Agnes became embroiled in a heated argument. The confrontation upset Agnes so much that she started throwing dishes around, breaking furniture, tearing pictures and threatening her husband. John felt the argument was getting out of control, so he decided to leave his wife alone for a few hours to allow her to calm down. John went to work at his broom maker's shop, which he operated in partnership with Bill Hookey. When he returned home at one p.m., his wife was still angry and refused to speak to him.

John's efforts to defuse the situation failed. He decided to lie down and have a nap. At three o'clock he left the house to visit his mother on William Street. Still bothered by his wife's outburst of violent behaviour, John discussed the incident with his mother. Mrs. Conroy offered to go and talk with Agnes on John's behalf. John agreed and they both set out for Mundy Pond together. As they neared the Conroy residence, John stopped to visit Bill Hookey, but his mother went on alone. When she arrived at the house, she found the front door locked and her heavy pounding on the door failed to get a response. Concerned by this, Mrs. Conroy called for her son, and, after attempting to open the front door, he went to the rear of the house and forced entry through the back door. His mother followed.

A horrible scene greeted the two. They began to cry and scream. The commotion attracted the attention of neighbours who began rushing to their aid. They were shocked to see, lying in a pool of blood on the kitchen floor, Agnes Conroy and her two daughters, three year old Ethel and six month old Sarah. All three had their throats slit. Sarah's throat had been slit by two deep incisions extending half way round the neck. Ethel lay beside her mother with her head facing the door. Her throat was cut from ear to ear. Neighbours helped John and his mother settle down then sent for the police and a doctor.

When the police arrived John was again hysterical. He cried bitterly as Dr. Taite and Dr. Keegan examined the bodies. John kept repeating, "My darlings, my darlings are gone." It was just the day before the slayings that the Conroy's celebrated Ethel's third birthday.

Dr. Tait determined that the two children were dead, but Agnes was still alive. When the police wagon arrived she was placed on board and rushed to the General Hospital.

The *Telegram*'s report of the incident stated, "Two innocent infants have been put into eternity by the hand of their jealous mother, who afterwards tried to take her own life but failed in the attempt." Inspector O'Reilly led the police investigation into what they suspected was a murder-suicide attempt by the children's twenty-six-year-old mother. It was believed that Agnes had cut her own windpipe and doctors held little hope that she would recover.

Following several days' treatment at the General Hospital on Forest Road she was removed to the Penitentiary, where she never regained consciousness. Agnes lived for two months after the murder and finally succumbed to her self-inflicted wounds on September 13, 1895.

Headlines in the *Telegram* read;" Agnes Conroy Dead — Gone To Be Tried By The Greatest Tribunal Of All." The story read, "Agnes Conroy will never stand trial for taking the lives of her two children. She died in Her Majesty's Penitentiary at 6:30 a.m. on September 13. Her death comes as a relief to the community. 'Better dead', is the comment of everyone."

May 12, 1899
Murdered in New Gower St. Tavern

Francis Canning, owner of a New Gower St. Tavern, enjoyed an ordinary, quiet and happy family life at his home on Theatre Hill (now Queen's Road). Then, in 1898, Francis began having severe headaches which caused him to fight with other family members. He used to enjoy the music provided by his son and daughter who played the piano and violin for him. But when suffering from the headaches he would swear and order that no music be played in the house. Francis would stay up all night and toss dishes around the kitchen and at anyone present.

The neighbourhood butcher noted the change. He recalled Canning sitting on the chopping block in his store and then suddenly jumping up and shouting, "I'm in a nut shell." Dooley later told the Court, "Canning looked scared and shocking, like a man just out of the asylum."

About a year after Canning's headaches began, Mary Nugent, the twenty-year-old barmaid at Canning's tavern, became engaged. She was planning to move into an apartment on Pleasant Street near her close friend Mary Tracy. At around three p.m. on May 12, 1899, Mary Tracy went to Canning's to get a drink of brandy for her sick child. As her hand touched the tavern door knob she heard three gunshots. Cautiously entering, she heard a woman crying, "Oh my! Oh my! Oh my!" Suddenly Canning appeared at the head of the stairs and shouted, "What do you want?"

Mrs. Tracy quivered as she replied,"Two glasses of spirits." Canning served the drinks and told her to beat it. Frightened, she fled the scene. A man working nearby responded to her cry for help and went to the tavern in time to see Canning leave. The man, Bill Brazil, said he could hear a woman crying from the upstairs and when he went to investigate saw Mary Nugent lying on the floor with her face covered in blood. Brazil called the police.

Mary was still alive when police arrived. A white substance believed to be from the brain had oozed from the wound onto the floor. When they moved her, she vomited. The Doctor arrived and poured a drink of brandy into the victims's mouth. When Inspector General McCowan asked, "Who did this?" the victim moaned, "Jesus, Mary and Joseph pray for me." A puff like smoke shot up from the wound. The girl was taken to the old General Hospital.

When police arrested Canning he told them that the shooting was an accident. He said he and Nugent were arguing. She lost her temper and grabbed a revolver. He struggled with her to take it away and it went off three times. One of the bullets hit Nugent and she fell to the floor. Police took Canning to Mary Nugent's bedside. She recognized him and didn't appear to be angry. She asked him why he had not been down to see her earlier.

She then agreed to give police a statement. She stated that the two became involved in an argument after she told Canning she was leaving to get married. Canning was against her doing this. She said:

> The day I was shot, Canning made no attempt to take liberties with me. I never quarrelled as bad as I did that time with anyone. Had no warning I was going to be shot. Half of my hat got torn while I tried to take it from Canning. He had it in his hand. I think he did not want me to go away. I have an awful temper. Think I told him I wanted to go away. He didn't want me to. Think I told him I was going to be married.

Mary Nugent told police that Canning was acting strange for months before the incident she reported "I told Mrs. Canning he was off his head or something strange was the matter with him two weeks ago." Before leaving the hospital, Canning shook hands with Nugent and they wished each other well. Several days later, Mary Nugent passed away.

On the day of the shooting the doctors failed to retrieve all of the bullet and a piece of it had lodged in a bone near the brain. Had doctors been able to remove the fragment, the girl would have lived. Canning was charged with murder.

The defence put up a strong effort to show Canning was insane. Over ten witnesses, all close friends and associates of Canning, testified to his very strange behaviour over the 12 months leading up to the killing. Two psychiatrists, one of them the head of the Hospital for Mental and Nervous Diseases, told the Court that Canning was insane. The theme of the defence was that Canning suffered severe headaches, loss of appetite, insomnia and violent fits, during which he tossed items at whoever came near him. Canning's oldest son, Arthur, testified that on the night before the shooting his father was talking to himself, acting very strange and was upset. I thought he was drunk or had lost his mind." Other evidence showed Canning had suffered sun stroke several years earlier while travelling to Brazil.

Dr. Tait, head of HMND, told the court there was proof beyond doubt that Canning was insane. He said he was suffering from 'megrim,' a condition brought on by sunstroke or heavy drinking. Tait's evidence was supported by Dr. McKenzie, also from the Mental Hospital.

The prosecution based its case on the victim's statement given before she died, the letter and statement of the accused admitting guilt, and testimony of Dr. Rendell of the General Hospital. Dr. Rendell, although not a psychiatrist, disputed psychiatric evidence and argued that Canning's behaviour was brought on by heavy drinking. He explained, "Irritability of temper is caused by excessive drinking and the mind might still be clear." Psychiatry was a little understood field in 1899 and, unfortunately for Canning, more credibility was attached to Dr. Rendell's opinion.

It was customary at that time for the accused to give an oral statement to the Court. While Canning's lawyer's objected, the judge insisted. Canning in a quivering voice and with body trembling testified, "Only after the action I awakened to a dim consciousness that some calamity had occurred to her and that I had been connected with it. I have never been conscious of any feelings towards Mary Nugent except of kindness and respect. She was an honest and faithful employee. I advised her not to be too hasty about getting married. She was very young and the whole world would be before her. She was like a daughter to me." In conclusion he showed remorse and begged for forgiveness for what he had done.

The defence lawyer reminded the jury of the friendly relations between Nugent and Canning as evidenced at the hospital visit by Canning to the victim.

The jury deliberated for four hours and returned a guilty verdict. Canning burst into tears and cried out, "Oh my God, I am innocent!" Canning's friends joined members of the clergy in a petition to stop the hanging. But Governor McCallum consulted with the judges of the Supreme Court and refused to commute the sentence.

The night before he was hung, Canning sat and talked with his wife, two children and his sister-in-law in his cell. The family left at 10:30 p.m. and at 11:00 p.m. Canning was given a snack of tea and toast.

At 7:45 a.m. next morning, amid one of the worst thunder and lightning storms witnessed in this city, the bells of the prison began to toll. Dressed in an ordinary black suit and wearing slippers, Canning had his arms pinioned to his side as the execution procession prepared to escort him to the gallows. At 7:55 the priests began the Litany for the Dead and the death procession started. Canning prayed every step of the way. The prisoner walked firmly to the gallows, fulfilling his promise not to flinch. Warden Fleet arranged the noose around Canning's neck and instructed him to step on the trap door with his face looking north.

The executioner, a prison inmate, wore long rubbers, a brown overcoat, greyish pants and a black woolen cap pulled over his face. His five-foot-five, 155 pound frame approached Canning and pulled a black cap down over Canning's face. Just before the executioner released the bolt, Canning prayed, "Lord, have mercy on my soul. Into thy hands O Lord, I commend my spirit. Lord have mercy on my soul."

A flash of lightning followed by a clap of thunder marked the descent of Francis Canning into the jaws of the gallows. Priests and nuns throughout the city were completing their twenty-four hours of prayer for the condemned man while hundreds of curious city residents braved the storm to try and get a glimpse of the execution.

The one inch thick manila rope, suspended from a beam twelve feet above the gallows, stretched five inches with the weight of Canning's body as it tightened violently around his throat extracting the last breath from the condemned man.

Witnesses in the prison yard were oblivious to the torrential rainstorm raging around them as they stood in silence, weeping. The final drama in the Canning case had been acted out and his body was cut down and buried thirty feet from the gallows. His last wish was that the press ask the public not to discuss his hanging anymore for the sake of his wife and children. He said, "I have paid with my life the full penalty for what I have done."

Four

Early Twentieth Century

July 4, 1903
The Cape Broyle Murder

*A*round the turn of the century it was not uncommon for captains of fishing vessels operating on the Grand Banks to carry a revolver. Captain Francis Woolard of the banker *Helen Whitten* was a little different in this respect. While he owned a revolver and kept it on board ship, he rarely carried it with him—with one fatal exception.

Woolard had fished on the Banks for 27 years, and 1903 experienced his most difficult time. Nine crew members deserted, which delayed sailing each time in order to find replacements. Two men were lost in the fog on the St. Lawrence. They were rescued but did not return to Woolard's vessel. On the Banks two more were lost in the fog: Pat Yetman and Joe Penney. They were picked up by a French vessel and dropped off at Bay Bulls. The two went from there to Cape Broyle and returned to work with Woolard. By this time Woolard had an inexperienced crew which resulted in a much smaller catch of fish than usual.

Captain Woolard gave Yetman a dollar and sent him to
Caplin Cove* to recruit a new worker. Crewman Joe Walsh,
a tall, heavy-set, powerful man witnessed the transaction.
Wollard later described to police what happened then:
"Walsh asked for money and I said, 'I have no money.' He
put his hand around my neck and tried to put his hand in my
vest pocket. I shoved him away. He said if that's what you
want I'll give you enough of it." Walsh then struck Woolard
in the face, knocking him to the ground. Woolard said, "No,
I don't want to fight."

Captain Woolard went to Sir Michael Cashin's office and
described what happened. Cashin called Constable Green
and Woolard made an assault complaint against Walsh.
While giving his statement he said, "If he hits me again, I will
shoot him." Cashin suggested that it would be wiser if the
captain gave Walsh twenty-five dollars to return home to
Nova Scotia.

Because of the difficulty of getting a crew, Woolard chose
to keep Walsh on board. The Captain was anxious to increase
his catch but was deeply concerned over his own safety. He
was even more concerned when Walsh confronted him saying, "You tried to do me dirty yesterday. You tried to get clear
of me.But I'll get square with you." Woolard ignored the
threat and ordered Walsh to go forward and "Heave up
anchor." Walsh retorted, "Ill go when I get Goddamn good
and ready."

Walsh then raised the issue that Yetman was threatening
to desert the ship. The Captain replied, "If he leaves this
vessel, he leaves dead." Yetman ignored the threat and got
into a dory to leave. Woolard pulled his revolver and ordered

---

*   Now known as Calvert.

Yetman back on ship. Yetman answered by shouting, "Go to Hell!" Walsh mischievously asked Wollard, "What are you scared of? Shoot!" Wollard recalled, "I fired then, right straight out from where I stood. Yetman rose up with a knife in hand." Woolard again fired several rounds. One of them split Yetman's heart in half and killed him.

Captain Woolard showed no remorse after the shooting, but ordered the crew to set sail. Instead, they went ashore and returned with the police. Walsh then attempted to prevent the police from taking the Captain. He refused to give them the gun which he had taken from Woolard. When they moved to arrest the Captain he singlehandedly fought the three policeman. The Head-Constable had to use his baton to knock out Walsh. Woolard then stepped forward and offered no resistance.

Woolard's comments, however, indicated he was in a state of confusion. He talked about having shot Walsh, claiming he had planned and intended to shoot Walsh. He was taken to St. John's to stand trial on murder charges. Meanwhile, at Ferryland, Walsh was convicted of assault and sentenced to six months at HMP. In passing sentence the judge said he regretted he could not put Walsh in Woolard's place. He argued, "You unhinged his mind and caused him to carry a revolver. You, through the instrumentality of the captain, practically fired the shot that killed Yetman and upon your head is Yetman's blood. The unfortunate captain has to go on trial for his life, but I can only give you six months."

Woolard's trial started on August 6, 1903. Because he was an American citizen a jurisdictional certificate had to be obtained from the Governor of Massachusetts under the Territorial Waters Act, 1878.

There was no doubt that Woolard killed Yetman. However, the defence put forward the argument that the shooting was a lawful act by the Captain against a crewman committing a crime. The defence claimed that the gun was used to prevent the crimes of felony, robbery and piracy.

The jury returned with a verdict of manslaughter and Captain Woolard was sentenced to 16 years at HMP. Dr. Freebain, who had performed the autopsy, shook Woolard's hand and said, "I hoped for a lesser sentence, but I'm glad it came out so well." Woolard answered, "Yes, but it's a terrible long sentence. I won't be much good for anything when i get out."

Captain Woolard was released from prison due to illness after serving six years. He returned to his family in the United States.

September, 1903
Harbour Main Graveyard

"**A** crime practically unknown in criminal history," is how the Prosecutor described the atrocity committed by James Murphy of Harbour Main. Murphy's insane love for Elizabeth Fewer drew him like a magnet to the graveyard near the Parish Church at Harbour Main on a dark September night in 1903. Elizabeth, the only love of his life, had passed away and been buried earlier that week in the church yard cemetery.

While Murphy had been madly in love with the attractive Elizabeth, she certainly didn't return that feeling. Just a year before her death, Elizabeth had married another man. Following the marriage Murphy tried to forget Elizabeth but his love for her was much too strong.

When she became sick and passed away, Murphy was both heartbroken and angry. On that dark September night, Murphy took a shovel and axe from his house and headed for the graveyard. Sarah Corbett of Chapel's Cove met and greeted Murphy near Hawco's house, just one hundred and fifty yeards from Murphy's residence. Murphy was unfriendly and barely replied to Sarah's greeting.

It was 9:00 p.m. and darkness had settled over the landscape when Murphy slowly walked through the cemetery, stopping at Elizabeth's grave. Using the axe and shovel he had brought with him, Murphy began to shovel the clay from the dead girl's grave. Once the top of the coffin was exposed, Murphy opened the coffin. Why he did what he did then, he couldn't really explain later, except to tell the judge, "The devil was at my side that night, urging me to go on."

Murphhy reached down inside the coffin and dragged Elizabeth from her final resting place. At first he began tearing her clothing away. This was followed by a savage attack upon the body with a knife. Murphy concluded his barbarous act by attempting to have intercourse with the corpse. During this activity a rock fell into the coffin. When Murphy tossed the body back into the coffin it rolled face down and struck the rock. The impact disfigured her face.

The next morning a visitor to the graveyard discovered the open grave and was shocked by the spectacle. Police were notified and before the end of the day they had arrested James Murphy.

When Murphy appeared in court he had no legal defence. The crown prosecutor was Justice Minister C.H.Hutchings. The jury was selected with no challenges being made by either side. A witness in the case was Michael Flynn, a neighbour and friend of James Murphy. He testified, "I remember the funeral. The day after I was called by Murphy and I went to the graveyard. The cover of the coffin was in pieces. There was a false cover with broken corners. I saw the body in the coffin face down. I turned the body over and took a rock out of the coffin. Elizabeth's chest was cut. Her nose was flattened. The clothes were torn from her breast and left in a heap. We covered up the body with a sack."

Inspector John Sullivan, the police officer who arrested Murphy, said that when he arrived there, the grave was still open and the body exposed. He said there were two cuts forming a cross that had been made on the body with a knife. Sullivan noted that when he questioned Murphy about the deed, Murphy quickly admitted guilt.

There was no lawyer in court to argue that Murphy was insane. There were no doctors or psychiatrists to testify that the accused was mentally ill. James Murphy defended himself in court. He admitted to the crime. In court he faced the experts of the justice system, trained lawyers, expert police witnesses and of course a well qualified and objective judge.

When the trial ended, the court found Murphy guilty as charged. He was sentenced to sixteen years in prison.

July 24, 1906

Policeman Attacked

To be a police officer in St. John's during the early days of this century required courage and strength. There were no two-way radios to call for help, no guns in the trunk of the car—no car. Police officers of the era were usually tall, powerful and fearless men. One police officer who epitomized the profession was Constable Stapleton. Many stories were told of his heroics and his humorous contacts with some of the well known characters of the town, like the famous Mickey Quinn.

One story, which would send chills up the spine of even an armed policeman, was based on a true encounter between Stapleton and a madman on Military Road in 1906. The Evening Telegram reported the incident on July 24, 1906 under the headline "Attacked With a Pick Axe." It read:

"Hugh Walsh, a labourer of the East End became insane on Rawlin's Cross yesterday afternoon and attacked Constable Stapleton with a pick axe. He made a blow at the officer's head, and had it connected it would undoubtedly have killed him. It was an unpleasant moment for the officer, but there was nothing left for him to do but wrestle with his infuriated opponent. Walsh is a burly man, and one not easy overpowered.

"Fortunately for Stapleton, he succeeded in grasping the axe; he endeavoured to take it, but found it too heavy a task, as Walsh was bent on destruction and would not give it up. After some minute of desperate struggling, the Constable, by Herculean strength, managed to tear it from the madman and fling it out of harms way. Walsh then fought with his fists, but being minus the pick axe the officer felt in better humour to contend with him.

"Walsh, however, was not to be easily overcome, and he worked like a demon. Stapleton's hope was to handcuff him, but this was more than he could do alone. He succeeded in throwing him to the ground and held him until Cornelius Pender and a couple of others happened along to his assistance.

"Hughie struggled, but notwithstanding the bracelets

were adjusted, but a minute later he pulled his hands through. Similar trouble was experienced in putting them on the second time, but they completed the job, and calling a cab drove their man to the police station.

"Upon reaching the door Walsh showed fight once again, and two other officers were necessary to carry him into the station. He was laid on the floor, and kicked the men as they put on a strait jacket.

"Sgt.Corbett was on guard and barely escaped being bitten by the frenzied man. They also found it necessary to bind his feet before putting him in the cell. It was a sad sight to witness the unfortunate. Being unable to do the police hurt, he pounded his head on the floor with terrible force three or four times. His cries could be heard for blocks away." Dr. Rendell arranged for the prisoner to be taken to the Hospital for Mental and Nervous Diseases. The Telegram concluded, "Constable Stapleton is to be congratulated on his escape; had he been less courageous, perhaps, he would not be as sound in limb today."

During another, more amusing incident, Stapleton matched wits with the town character Mickey Quinn. Quinn was resting in a boarding house on Williams Lane when a friend rushed in to tell him that a large crate full of bologna had broken on the wharf. The friend told Mickey that Stapleton was standing guard over the scattered property until it could be accounted for and re-crated.

Quinn accepted a bet from the others in the home that he could not penetrate the security on the wharf to steal a bologna.

In minutes, Quinn was standing on the wharf sizing up the situation. Sure enough, the bologna was spread all over the place, but under the watchful eye of Constable Stapleton, Quinn eluded the policeman and got onto the wharf. However, when he attempted to leave the area with an obvious bulge sticking out from his overcoat, Stapleton stopped him and asked what he was hiding.

Quinn replied, "Nothing only me pet cat. She ran down the wharf and I found her near the bologna."

Stapleton: "You think I was born yesterday, Quinn? Open your coat!"

Quinn: "I'd rather not, sir, because she might get away."

Stapleton: "I insist. You open your coat right now or I'll take you to the lockup."

Quinn:"All right, sir." As he opened the coat, out jumped a big black tomcat and ran down the wharf. Stapleton, red faced, apologized to Quinn and told him to go find his cat.

Minutes later Quinn, again leaving the wharf with his coat bulging out, encountered Stapleton. This time Stapleton commented, "I see you found your cat, Mickey." To which Quinn replied, "Thank the Lord," and continued to walk up the street.

When he arrived at the boarding house he shouted to his friends, "Well I done it. I got the bologna, now pay up."

Opening his coat he pulled out a full bologna. But Quinn was surprised at the lack of enthusiasm showed by his buddies.

Then he heard a loud meow. When he turned he saw that the black cat had followed him, and Constable Stapleton had followed the black cat. The police officer recovered the stolen bologna and Mickey found himself cooling off in the lockup.

September 5, 1906

Prison Escape

On September 5, 1906, eighteen-year-old Philip Brady, an English immigrant living in St. John's, was sentenced to Her Majesty's Penitentiary for eighteen months after being found guilty of stealing money from the Dunphy family at Holyrood. Six weeks later he was on his way to becoming Newfoundland's first criminal folk hero.

Just two months into his sentence Brady yearned for the outside and began planning his escape. He enlisted the help of cell mate John Farrell. Two of the main centres of prisoner activity at the pen were the industrial room and the broom room where inmates were taught the art of broom making. Brady's plan involved stealing a rope from the Industrial room and using it to scale the walls while the guards were not on watch. To get the rope outside, he hid it in a barrel of slop near the kitchen. Later, he helped other prisoners take the barrels outside to dump the contents and he made sure the rope was covered with slop so the watching guards would not detect it.

At 5:30 pm when the inmates were locked up, Brady and Farrell asked permission to go to the toilet and were escorted there by a guard. The two escaped to the outside from the toilet area crossed over along the roof and jumped down to the garbage dump. They retrieved the rope, then dashed towards the lower end of the prison and hid in a turnip patch. When they felt safe, they moved to the corner of the wall and tossed the rope over. Brady went over the wall first, but before Farrell had a chance to move he was scared off by the prison dogs and captured by the guards. It was now dark and the warden ordered guards to search the prison and Quidi Vidi area. He also alerted local police.

After a reward was posted police were flooded with reports that Brady had been sighted. The most promising one came from Paddy Coughlan of Heavy Tree Road. He claimed Brady broke into his house, robbed clothing and food, and left. Paddy had Brady's prison clothes to support his claim. The police searched the area but Brady was gone.

The next day, the search shifted to Manuels. Police followed a tip that Brady was on the railway tracks in that area. The two police officers caught up with the suspect but he was the wrong man.

The search then shifted to Pleasantville. Inspector McCowan received a call that a hotel owner in that area was holding the fugitive in his home. By that time all the police were in the countryside searching and McCowan had to call on the Fire Department for help. By the time McCowan and the two firemen arrived on the scene they were joined by two policemen. The owner took great delight in explaining how he had singlehandedly persuaded Brady to come into his house.

McCowan and four men rushed into the kitchen where the suspect was having lunch. However, the blond haired man was not the least perturbed. He looked at the police and smiled and continued eating his meal. McCowan said, "He's not Brady." The man turned out to be Paul Gorman, a retarded adult well known around the City. Gorman bore a strong resemblance to Philip Brady, a fact which complicated the police search.

The next day the police followed another lead to Manuels and instead of finding Brady, again picked up Paul Gorman. The manhunt drew much publicity and the police received and followed up dozens of tips. One such tip lead them to ambush a man eating lunch on a schooner in St. John's Harbour. The man turned out to be a well-known City bum. A search of the Blackhead area turned up a Danish sailor and two German sailors.

By now the police were the subject of jokes and wise-cracks among the public. This angered Inspector General McCowan. So when he received a telegram that police had arrested Brady at Brigus and were bringing him back to St. John's that afternoon on the Newfie Bullet he helped spread the word of the success. By the time the train arrived in St. John's crowds of spectators had flooded the railway station to get a glimpse of the famous criminal. When the train pulled in the police drew the horse drawn police wagon to the arrival platform. Soon, two police officers escort a blond-hair, hand-cuffed man from the train. The man looked out over the crowd and smiled. The crowd roared laughing. It was the retarded gentleman, Paul Gorman, now arrested for the third time. This time however, McCowan met with Gor-man's father and asked that he be kept of the streets until Brady was recaptured.

On November 2, Paddy Coughlan from Heavy Tree Road came to the police station and insisted on speaking to Inspec-tor-General McCowan. He claimed he had been robbed again and refused to meet with anyone other than the Inspector-General. When told McCowan was not available he left in a huff.

Superintendent Sullivan took two police officers and went to Paddy's to conduct another search. Paddy was not at home so they searched the fields and barns. When Paddy returned he accused the police of robbing him and searching his property without a proper warrant. He shouted, " The police search my house at all hours of the day and night without as much as a 'by your leave,' sir. They have no warrant, and when I complain to them they threaten me with hand cuffs. They have a grudge against me and I don't want them around. They are not the least bit courteous to me." He said with Brady in the area he hid one hundred dollars in bills in his cellar and the police watched him do it then stole the money.

Letters began appearing in the press poking fun at the police. One letter in the Evening Telegram on November 2, 1906 read: "Will you do me the favour to ask your readers if they can inform me if the report is correct that Mr. Brady, who for some time had been a guest at the Hotel de Parsons (HMP) on the Sir Edward Morris Boulevard, has been sending post cards to his detective friends and a copy of his photo to be enlarged and hung in the dining halls of the hotel and that his health is good and that there is no need for the least anxiety on his account." The letter closed by asking, "Where is our wandering boy tonight?" Another letter suggested a public concert with Superintendent Sullivan singing, "Phil Brady, will you please come home?"

A poem also appeared in the press which city people sang to the tune of "My Irish Molly Oh." Part of it read:

Now Willies dear, and did you hear
The news that's down the street
Young Brady has escaped from jail
He did it rather neat.
The jailers are all nearly wild
Their grief is awful sad
Because they've lost their darling boy
Their little English lad.
Oh Brady wise, you fooled us boys
And left us in a trance
Filled up with holy horrors cause
You stole Pad Coughlan's pants

They're rather big, and so, you pig
A glutton you must be
Or else yo'd never take size eight
When you want but a three.

On November 14, 1906, in a desperate move, the police decided to conduct a search in the Kilbride area. Brady had worked on Brennan's farm and knew that area well. The search paid off. Constable Mackey, about ready to give up noticed a shadow moving down in Densmore's potato cellar. He looked down and commented, "Well, hello Brady." Brady tried to fight his way out using a pitch fork but he was subdued by Mackey and Savage who hand cuffed him and escorted him to town in a police wagon. He had been free for 71 days.

Word of the capture spread quickly and by the time the police got to the cross-roads hundreds of people had lined the streets to get a glimpse of the famous escapee. Brady told McCowan he read the papers while on the run and was amused at the shenanigans of police in trying to find him. He said he didn't think the Newfoundland police were as smart as the Scotland yard boys and , "I outsmarted them too."

Brady served 16 months and was released on March 5, 1908. He died a few years later of TB and was buried in Mount Carmel Cemetery near the tall cross where he had hidden on his first night after escaping prison.

September 21, 1907

On September 21, 1907, the body of a headless man was found at Gull Marsh, Bonne Bay. there were two holes in the chest three inches below the collar bone. His clothes were saturated in blood. The head of the body was never found and the man was never identified.

January 1, 1908

Newfoundlander Murdered in Jamaica

A young Newfoundlander named Lacey from La Scie was buried with full military honours on January 4, 1908 at Kingston, Jamaica.

Lacey was a crew member of the HMS *Brilliant*. On New Year's Day, 1908 the *Brilliant* was moored at Kingston Harbour, and Lacey was one of a number of crew members that went ashore to celebrate. He was quiet, but physically strong. He was also a teetotaller. While his buddies went drinking, Lacey visited a Temperance House with another friend and teetotaller.

Word reached Lacey that his buddies had gotten into a row with a group of Jamaicans in a saloon next door and three of them had been severely beaten. Lacey rushed to their assistance. When he arrived, a friend was being beaten up by the natives. Lacey didn't hesitate. He immediately waded into the fray, swinging and kicking as he tried to rescue his shipmate.

The racket lasted about fifteen minutes, then the Jamaicans pulled knives and began slashing at the helpless Newfoundlander. By the time the police arrived young Lacey was covered with blood and dying. He was taken aboard the *Brilliant* and given medical treatment. Thirty-eight hours later he died. He was only twenty years old when murdered.

January 15, 1908
Assyrian Feud on Water Street

Dominic Richards didn't kill anybody. Neither did he fire any of the shots into two fellow countrymen who lay beside him in a pool of blood. But Dominic Richards stood trial in connection with the shooting incident and Dominic Richards was found guilty and sent to prison at Her Majesty's Penitentiary, St. John's.

The flare-up that ended in five bullets being fired, three men lying on the floor covered in blood, and Richard Joseph running for his life up Water Street, took place on January 15, 1908 in the kitchen of Annie George's house. Annie operated a store and boarding house on Water Street; she and all her boarders were Assyrian immigrants. (In those days, Assyrian immigrants took English names to blend in with the local community.) Every night after supper, other Assyrian friends would visit and play cards.

Among those playing cards that night were Annie's friends Basil Noah and Maleem Noah. Richard Joseph of George Street and Dominic Richards, who lived with his wife and two children at Norris Arm, arrived while the game was in progress. Tension filled the room because all present knew of the feud between Basil Noah and Dominic Richards, which had started several days earlier at the nearby Strong's Saloon. The two had been involved in a fist fight which left Richards determined to seek revenge.

Dominic had an almost hypnotic influence over his younger friend Richard Joseph. After the saloon fight, he told Joseph, "We will kill him. God damn them all. You got no blood in you Joseph. Shoot him. You got to kill him."

Dominic later purchased a gun and bullets and began manipulating Joseph into shooting Noah.

Earlier on the fateful day of January 5, Dominic, who was visiting St. John's on business, was a guest at Richard Joseph's home. The two went out and spent the day visiting friends and drinking. Joseph's wife later told police that she found the two at Dominic's sister's house with several liquor bottles on the table. Dominic was saying, "Drink away boy, drink and do not be afraid. I will give my life for you and my blood also." Then striking his clenched fist on the table said, "I have 2,000 pounds and don't give a damn; there's one thousand for you and one thousand for me."

She didn't know what he meant by the statement.

When Joseph's wife tried to get him to go home, Dominic became angry and shouted at Joseph, "Are you a damn fool to listen to a woman?" He told Mrs. Joseph to take her child home and leave Joseph alone.

Dominic and Joseph turned up at Annie's just as the nightly card game had started. Dominic was loud and insulting. Basil Noah, who later said he felt that Dominic and Noah had come to start a fight, ordered him to behave or be put out, and a fist fight started. Dominic wrestled Basil Noah to the floor. At this point Richard Joseph pulled a revolver from his pocket and fired five times in rapid succession. The first bullet hit the ceiling. The second struck Maleem Noah, and the third hit Basil Noah. Two other shots penetrated the walls. Others might have been hit if Wattie Murphy, Annie's boarder, had not grabbed the gun from Joseph. During the turmoil, Dominic Richards pretended to have been shot.

Richard Joseph fled the house; Annie George screamed at him that he had killed three men. She said, "You will run now. But you won't get clear when the police come." Annie then called the police.

Meanwhile, Joseph ran into own his house shouting, "Oh my God! Dominic Richards is after passing his tricks on me and ruined me. What is he going to do for me now?" Minutes later the police were at the door. His lips were white and his face looked strained as they arrested him. Two police officers took him back to the crime scene. The two wounded men still lay on the floor waiting on medical attention.

When Noah saw Joseph he said in a weak voice, "That is the man who shot me. Kill him for me. Shoot him." Neighbours had to restrain Noah's friends or they would have attacked Joseph. Shortly after, the injured men were taken to hospital where they recovered from their wounds.

Both Dominic and Joseph were charged in connection with the double shooting. While Joseph was charged with the shooting, his friend Dominic was charged with, "unlawfully encouraging one Richard Joseph feloniously and wilfully and of malice aforethought to murder one Noah Basil Noah and Maleem Noah." Dominic denied owning the gun or having ever purchased it.

Although the victims survived the shooting, their assailants did not escape justice. They were both sentenced to seven years at the Newfoundland Penitentiary. Less than a month later, both men attempted suicide.

March 25, 1908

Murder Near Buchanan Street

*T*he names Holy Arch and Back of the Sun have long disappeared from the scene in St. John's, but there was a time when they were household names in the City. On March 25, 1908, they made newspaper headlines across Newfoundland when a man living at Holy Arch accused a man living at Back of the Sun of running a whore house.

Holy Arch was a narrow street exiting from Buchanan Street. Sixty-nine year old John Day with his wife and two children, one aged four years, the other 18 months, lived at Holy Arch. Adjoining Holy Arch, and almost a part of it, was Back of the Sun. Here lived Thomas Tobin, whose wife had passed away a few months earlier. He lived there with his four children and three female boarders.

John Day and his wife were good friends of young Tobin. When Mrs. Tobin passed away, Mrs. Day often cleaned house and did laundry for the Tobin family. She even cared for the Tobin children when Tobin and her husband sometimes went off to work together. But when Tobin took a young girl into his household, and shortly after, two more girls, John Day became suspicious. The presence of three young girls in the house so soon after the death of Tobin's wife seemed inappropriate.

Soon after the girls moved in, a steady stream of young men began visiting the house. On several occasions Day complained to Tobin but Tobin insisted there was nothing irregular going on at the house. On one occasion Tobin became upset with Day's complaints, and verbally abused the old man.

On the evening of March 25, 1908, Tobin had tea at home with one of the girls and two of his children. After supper, he went down to the King Edward Hotel on Water Street to "fire up," or have a few drinks. When he returned he took the grocery book and invited his 15 year old son Tom to come with him to the grocery store.

Tobin's son later said that when he and his father were passing through Holy Arch, while returning from the grocery store, Day confronted his father, claiming he was running a whore house. Mr. Tobin ran into his own house, threw off his coat and returned to continue the argument with Day.

The girl at Tobin's house told police, "When he came back, as soon as he entered the house he threw his coat on the floor and ran out cursing Day."

Gideon Way, a witness to the incident, stated: "I was going down Buchanan Street, and shouts emanating from the Holy Arch attracted my attention, and I ran in there. Tom Tobin and John Day had hold of each other. I saw Day strike Tobin with a walking stick. I separated them and told Tobin not to strike Day as he was an old man." Way then left.

Tom Tobin jr. said, "I saw Day strike my father with a walking stick. Way and Joe White were there also. My father then punched Day in the nose."

According to the witnesses, Day fell against a wall. Way broke up the fight and as Day was escorted to his own home by his four-year old son he shouted, "Tobin, this is a blow you will have to pay for." Day collapsed on the kitchen floor. His wife sent for Dr. Campbell who lived on New Gower Street. Campbell arrived minutes later, but too late to help Day, who was dead.

Less than an hour after the fight, a neighbour brought Tobin the news that Day was dead. When the seriousness of the situation hit Tobin he became ill and nearly collapsed. His ordeal went on for almost two months with remand after remand until finally his trial got underway.

Dr. Scully, who had performed the post-mortem, told the Court that Day's organs were diseased to the extent that he would have soon died anyway. The injury inflicted by Tobin resulted in a small bruise on the edge of Day's nose. The Doctor noted that the cause of death was the diseased condition of the arteries. They had been in a diseased condition before the fight. Dr. Scully acknowledged, however, that, "the blow would cause a certain amount of excitement, and that excitement acting upon a heart already overtaxed doing the work it had to do, would cause death."

The jury took only fifteen minutes to decide that Tobin was not guilty of manslaughter. There was great rejoicing at the Back of the Sun that night.

June 2, 1908

Children Jailed

A newspaper reporter walking along Water Street on June 2, 1908 was appalled by the sight of three children, ranging in age from eleven to thirteen, years being carted off by the local constabulary to Her Majesty's Penitentiary at St. John's. The 13 year old boy was sent to jail for leaving his job on a fishing vessel. He had been charged with and convicted of desertion. Another boy named McGrath was serving time for vagrancy while the remaining boy was jailed for theft.

The children were confined in the back of a horse drawn police cart with three adult convicts, one of whom was a man convicted of attempted murder. The sight of the little children crying and pleading to be released attracted the attention of many people that day. But the citizens, police and prison guards could do little to help. They were victims of a harsh justice system that treated children as adults.

The reporter stated:"To see boys being dragged along with such characters was a disgrace to the community, and only once again demonstrates the need for a reformatory." Demands for a children's reformatory were frequently made by people outraged by this form of justice. Several days after these children were jailed, a ten year old boy named Woodley was arrested by police and sent to prison. He had stolen cigarettes from Annie George's store on Water Street and was caught by police as he puffed on a cigarette in a Water Street laneway.

Unlike the other three children, he was not given the luxury of a ride to prison. The boy, along with five adult prisoners, was forced to march along Water Street to the prison. The lad was wearing ragged clothes and had no shoes. The Daily News reported, "Such a scene is a disgrace in the chief town of Britain's oldest colony and the need for a reformatory was once more strongly demonstrated."

William Kendall, a volunteer worker at the prison, was repulsed by the scene of youngsters crying and being forced into cells with adult prisoners. He wrote a letter to the local papers which read, "Among the lads there was one poor little fellow only 11 years old. His little baby face was the very picture of guilessness and innocence, his cries were heart rending. He pleaded that if they would let him out he would never do it again, but of course, the officials had no power to release him and there he was, little older than a baby, behind bars."

The child shared a cell with an adult convict. Kendall continued, "While making enquiries about him his eyes filled with tears, and his whole face was the picture of anguish and trouble. Your readers can form their own opinions of a system which consigns such as these to a common jail."

Others in St. John's favoured severe punishments for children who commited crimes. The following comments appeared in the Daily News in a letter signed, "Pro Bono." It read, " If some of these unfortunate youngsters got a good birching the first time they come up for petty larceny, or kindred offences, their names would never again appear on the police records. There are some natures and the only way to appeal to them is by causing physical suffering. They will cease their savagery for fear, when all other means fail. Many well-meaning but unthinking people will raise their hands in horror at this suggestion, but it is to people who know and who have had bitter experiences of the futility of ordinary methods, that the decision ought to be left.

"If a dozen strokes of a birch rod, humanely administered, taught a youngster who was disposed to evil ways either from heredity or environment, then the greatest kindness that the protection of public life and property could do to such, would be to stop depravity with corporal punishment."

The reformatory issue, coupled with the spectacle of children being jailed, touched the heart of a young boy who donated three dollars from his pocket money to start a fund for a reformatory. The Daily News stated, "The reformatory must come, and when it does it will be largely due to the fact that public opinion was effectually aroused by his gift. To thrust children into jail is to dedicate them to crime. Ever after they are known as the companions of thieves and murderers."

March 15, 1909

Who Was Jacques Millere?

One of the most long-standing unsolved mysteries in Newfoundland history involves the discovery of the body of a French man on the west coast of the province almost 90 years ago.

At 4pm on March 15,1909, Frank Penney found the body of a man named "Millere" on the grounds of the Humber River Pulp and Lumber Co. near Deer Lake. When the police arrived they searched the man's clothing and found some very intriguing documents.

The papers featured every conceivable kind of astronomical drawings and plans, as well as sketches of aircraft designs. In addition, police found writings which were highly imaginative descriptions of the planets and unusual philosophical dissertations on the relationship between humanity and the heavenly bodies.

The most amazing aspect of the discovered material was a post office receipt issued at Summerside, Prince Edward Island, showing that Jacques R. Millere had recently sent a registered letter to the Duke of Orleans in Paris.

Who was this Millere? One newspaper suggested he might have been some visionary royalist dreaming of the restoration of the French Monarchy or some scientific crackpot.

Despite police efforts to shed light on the Millere mystery, his secrets died with him. Millere was buried at the Catholic cemetery at Birchy Cove.

July 10, 1910
Newfoundlander charged in New York Murder

The discovery of a butchered twelve-year-old child in a vacant tenement lot at the Bronx, New York on July 10,1910 sparked a city-wide mobilization of police investigators, which led to the arrest of a young Newfoundlander.

Due to its brutality, the murder shocked New Yorkers and Newfoundlanders alike. The girl had been badly beaten, her hair was chopped off and there were repeated stab wounds over her upper body. New Yorkers were in a lynching mood.

Police moved swiftly to solve the crime and in less than forty-eight hours had a young Newfoundlander, Ernest Hottville, behind bars. Hottville had moved to New York from St. John's some years earlier with his family. He worked in the big city as a labourer. He lived in the same neighbourhood as the victim and matched the detailed eye-witness description of the man last seen with the girl.

At the precinct police station the young Newfoundlander was subjected to an intensive and gruelling interrogation at the hands of investigators. Police had searched Hottville for evidence but found nothing "of a suspicious nature." Apart from proclaiming his innocence, Hottville would not answer any of the police questions. He refused even to tell his address. Police were sure they had the killer.

Early next morning, with the Bronx courtroom filled with reporters, the accused monster killer was paraded in handcuffs to face the judge, where he was officially charged with the murder of Julia Connors. That evening New York papers reported the arrest and charging of the Newfoundlander. Newspapers described the killing as "a crime that passes comprehension."

A grand jury was convened and the wheels of justice moved rapidly. Within days the grand jury unanimously voted in favour of an "indictment of murder in the first degree." However, there was a surprise. It was not Ernest Hottville who was indicted.

An astonishing turn of events occurred on the second day of the court hearing which sent reporters scrambling out the doors to break the news. A distressed and despondent Hottville suddenly sat up alert and smiled at this favourable turn of fate.

The New York papers on July 16 described the episode, "Samuel Swartz, father of Nathan Swartz, a young hanger-on of pugilism who had been sought in connection with the crime, admitted to the grand jury that his son had confessed to him that he was guilty of killing the girl." This evidence was corroborated by another witness, Mrs. Frances Alexander, the sister of Nathan Swartz.

Mrs. Alexander's repetition of the story of the crime told to her by her brother, was detailed, explicit and telling in its revelation of horror. The witness testified that her brother had told her that he had met Julia Connors on Saturday night and asked her to take a pair of opera glasses to his home, which was just across the hall from the vacant flat where the murder was committed. The young man said he followed the girl, and at the top of the stairs pushed her into the flat and attempted to assault her. The child screamed, according to Mrs. Alexander, and then Nathan said he plunged his pocket knife into her. She continued to scream, the witness testified, and Nathan stabbed her until she finally fell and then he plunged the knife into her breast near the heart. Then Julia remained still.

Nathan went across the hall to his own apartment, the witness stated, and got the box in which the body was found. He placed the child, still alive, in the box, and after cutting off her hair, put the box on the dumbwaiter and let it slide to the basement.

Mrs. Alexander told the jury that Nathan said he went to the cellar and took the unconscious child from the dumbwaiter and laid her in the cellar. He then went home and went to sleep. Early the next morning (Sunday) he took the girl, still alive, into the lot where she was found.

The witness said she threw the youth out of her house when she heard the tale. He then went to his father's place of business where, according to evidence given by his father, he told the same story.

While records were not clear on what happened to Nathan Swartz, it was locally believed that he served a life sentence in a New York prison. Hottville walked out of the court room exonerated. For a short while his was a household name in New York City. But in time the travesty of justice committed against this young Newfoundlander was forgotten. The memory of the Hottville case has long since disappeared from the public mind.

1912

Smart Lawyer

During the summer of 1912 a man was being tried at Ferryland for stealing a friend's farm equipment. He pleaded not guilty and hired "a smart, gentleman lawyer from St. John's."

The complainant, a farmer named Cahill, had just been questioned by the prosecutor. The city lawyer smiled and leaning towards his client whispered, "No problem here." He began his strategic attack.

"You say that you can swear to having seen this man drive a horse past your farm on the day in question"

"I can," replied Cahill wearily, for he had already answered the question a dozen times for the Crown.

"What time was that?" queried the defence.

Cahill answered, "I told you it was about the middle of the forenoon."

"But I don't want any 'abouts' or any 'middles'!I want you to tell the jury exactly the time."

"Why?" asked Cahill. " I don't always carry a gold watch with me when I am digging potatoes."

"But you have a clock in the house, haven't you?" retorted the lawyer.

"Yes," answered the witness.

"Well, what time was it by that?" asked the lawyer.

"Well by that clock it was just nineteen minutes past ten," Cahill said.

"You were in the field all that morning?" the lawyer asked.

"I was" replied Cahill.

"How far from the house is the field?" the lawyer asked.

Cahill answered, "About half a mile."

"You swear, do you that by the clock in your house it was exactly nineteen minutes past ten?"

"I do" said Cahill

The lawyer paused and looked triumphantly at the jury. At last he had entrapped the old farmer into a statement that would greatly weaken his evidence.

"I think that will do," said the lawyer, with a wave of his hand. "I have quite finished with you."

Cahill leisurely picked up his hat and started to leave the witness box.

"I ought perhaps to say, yer honour," he added, "that too much reliance should not be placed on that clock as it gout out of gear about six months ago, and it's been nineteen minutes past ten ever since."

Old timers say that lawyer never again showed his face around the Shore.

September 12, 1912
The Killing of John Sears

John Duke and John Sears of St. John's were best friends. They attended the 1912 Regatta together and soon after signed on as ship mates on the *Lake Simcoe*. The vessel was to deliver a cargo to South America for Baine Johnston's Ltd.

Sears, the ship's captain Andrew Wilson, and most of the crew were aware that Duke displayed periodic bursts of violence and irrational behavior. During a trip in 1910, Duke, convinced the crew were plotting to murder him,had jumped over the side and had to be rescued by other crew members.

On the first day of the *Lake Simcoe*'s 29 day trip, Duke picked a fight with another crew member and was put in chains below deck for several days to sober up. Duke seemed more paranoid than usual and displayed a series of delusions.

On September 12 at around 5 am the weather was clear, the sea was quiet, and four seamen were on deck duty. Harvey Williams saw Duke coming out of the cabin. He watched him walk casually up to John Sears, seize him by the shoulder, wing him around and plunge a knife into the young man's throat.

Williams cried out "Murder! Murder!" He watched as Sears ran to the cabin, holding his throat. He recalled, "I went to call the Captain and saw a cut across John's throat about two and a half inches long." The stabbing cut the jugular vein and left a gash about two and a half inches long.

Before collapsing Sears cried out, "Oh Jesus, I'm filled." Meanwhile, Fred Nolan picked up an ax and faced Duke as he tried to gain entry into the cabin. Nolan said, "You son-of-a-bitch. You killed the boy." Duke replied, "I'm sorry I didn't get another dig at him." He then turned to the others and shouted, "Come on, every son-of-a-bitch on board."

Captain Wilson and the crew trapped Duke below deck. He gave up his knife after they swore on a prayer book they would not harm him. Wilson felt it would be safer to keep Duke below deck and not tell him of the death of Sears. They completed the delivery to South America and returned to St. John's harbour.

As Duke was being escorted from the ship a touching scene took place which stirred the emotions of all present and gained some momentary sympathy for the prisoner. Duke's wife Annie broke through the crowds, and rushing to her husband's side, grasped him tightly around the waist and burst into tears. Even Duke himself broke down and cried bitterly. Superintendent of Police Grimes interrupted the scene saying, "Let's go, we have to get you to the station." The police had not arranged transportation for the prisoner and their walk to the station was a public spectacle. Later that day, John Duke was charged with murder.

The issues at trial were clear. The defence argued insanity while the prosecution insisted that although Duke had not been drinking on the day of the murder, his insanity was brought on by his long term drinking. The defence called Dr. F.W. Scully from the Mental Hospital to explain how the DT's affected a person. Scully explained, "DT's or delirium tremens follow a drinking bout sometimes, or it may cause acute alcoholic insanity. A sudden fit of insanity might come on if a man who had been drinking heavily suddenly stops. It is quite possible for such a fit to come on several days after the subject had been quite well."

The defence also tried to show insanity in Duke's family. He introduced evidence that Duke's brother was mentally unstable because he had attempted suicide by jumping into St. John's Harbour a few years before. The defence also pointed out that Duke had an uncle who was a patient at the Mental Hospital.

When Duke took the stand he testified that he had no memory of killing anybody. However, he was aware that he had done something wrong. The defence summary argued that Duke had no motive to kill his friend. The defence suggested that the killing could only be explained by insanity, and there was strong evidence of insanity in the Duke family.

The prosecutor agreed that insanity was a defence but argued that the defence failed to prove that there was heredity insanity in Duke's case. The prosecutor stated, "We should not accept justification for murder by reason of insanity based on this evidence. Duke's behaviour was the result of alcohol rather than insanity. There are four kinds of insane people known to law; the idiot; the insane from fever; the lunatic with lucid intervals; and insanity from drinking."

The judge instructed the jury to consider only two questions: "First, Did the prisoner kill Sears?" and secondly, "Was the prisoner in such a state of mind as to not know what he was doing?"

The jury took just an hour to arrive at a verdict. He was found not guilty by reason of insanity. The judge ordered he be confined at the Waterford hospital, to be released, if at all, at the discretion of the Governor. Duke passed away at the hospital.

1919

Moonshiners

Chicago, New York and Boston were not the only hot spots during the prohibition years. There were many stills operating throughout Newfoundland, supplying the local market with illegal booze. The most notorious case of moonshining nearly led to an all-out war. To end the conflict, authorities had to call in a British warship, scores of marines and a squad of hefty cops.

This epic in our criminal history began in 1919, when police at St. John's received reliable reports that some people on Flat Island, Bonavista Bay, were illegally brewing intoxicants and distributing them indiscriminately. Authorities sent Constable John Summers to investigate the report, and at Greenspond he was joined by another constable.

The two proceeded to Flat Island. On nearby Coward Island they went ashore and searched five houses, but failed to turn up any evidence of moonshining. As they arrived at Flat Island they encountered three motor boats containing fifty men. Summers, an experienced police officer, took control of the situation. He stood up in the boat and identified himself, and began asking questions about the stills.

The police were told flatly to leave the area or be tossed into the water. Summers sensed they meant business and decided to avoid a confrontation at that time by returning to Greenspond. The moonshiners thought there would be no further threat from the man from St. John's. However, back in Greenspond, Summers telegraphed Police Inspector C.H.Hutchings. The inspector sent ten men to assist Summers in completing his investigation and enforcing the law.

A more confident Summers led the police unit to Flat Island, hoping to arrest the group leaders. When word spread that the police were back, people went to their homes and returned to the wharf armed with guns and ammunition.

They hid behind rocks and boulders and warned the police to leave "or be blown to hell." Outnumbered by nearly two hundred angry and armed people, Summers once again retreated. Once more he returned to Greenspond to seek help. He sent a second telegraph to the police inspector at St. John's, pleading for more help. Inspector Hutchings was determined that the law be obeyed at Flat Island and felt this would require extraordinary measures.

He called upon the HMS *Cornwall* which was visiting the port of St. John's and requested that its crew of British marines go to the assistance of his men at Greenspond.

The *Cornwall* picked up Summers and his men at Greenspond and launched a military assault at Flat Island which prompted one old-timer there to comment "the likes of it has never been seen around these parts before."

By this time most of the Flat Island men were away prosecuting the Labrador fishery. The remaining men offered no resistance and the assault team arrested seven ringleaders. A woman watching the spectacle became hysterical because she believed the marines were going to shoot her husband, one of the men who had been arrested. Another seven men returning from the Labrador fishery were arrested and were brought with the others to St. John's for trail.

Summers got his way. With the assistance of the Navy, he showed the Flat Island fisherment that they must respect those who enforce the law. However, amid the confusion and frustration of making the arrests, the police failed to gather needed evidence for the trial. This resulted in all the defendants being discharged. The Flat Islanders returned home and resumed moonshining.

The *Cornwall* also carried *Evening Telegram* reporter Joey Smallwood, later the premier of Newfoundland.

May 3, 1922
Triple Murder on Carter's Hill

The peaceful atmosphere of old St. John's was shattered on May 3, 1922 when news spread throughout town of a multiple slaying on Carter's Hill.*

The killing spree began with a dispute among four Chinese immigrants. Thirty-one-year-old Wo Fen Game worked at the Jim Lee Laundry for the three owners: Hong Loen, So Ho Kai and Hong Kim Hai. Kim Hai, who was Fen Game's brother-in-law, had loaned him the money to come here from China. He promised Fen Game work in the laundry at twelve dollars a week. Fen Game started at four dollars a week, then had his salary increased to eight dollars a week.

However, the laundry owners were not pleased with his work. Along with not meeting work requirements he began sleeping late and falling behind in his work. Finally, on May 3, they fired Fen Game. The Chinese community in the city were aware of the problems at the Jim Lee Laundry and on the day of the killings they sent Charlie Fong to mediate. Fong's efforts were fruitless; Hong Loen insisted that they would not take Fen Game back to work.

---

* In 1922 the top part of Carter's Hill was known as Murray Street

To Fen Game, this was a death sentence. He was in a strange country, unable to speak the language, and now that he was fired from the laundry he was shunned by other Chinese employers.

Fen Game had been expecting some kind of confrontation. The day before he had visited the Martin-Royal Stores on Water Street and purchased a .38 calibre nickel plated revolver which he hid in his bedroom over the laundry. After he was fired, he went to Loen and pleaded for another chance, claiming he was ready to commit suicide. Loen laughed and told Fen Game that he should kill himself because if he didn't, "me and Hong Wing will have to shoot you sometime." Hong Wing, co-owner of another Chinese laundry, had come from a rival village to Fen Game's. Family feuds had gone on between the two villages for years.

With tears in his eyes, Fen Game rushed up to his room, loaded his gun and returned to the laundry. His first victim was Hong Loen. After being shot, he crawled out onto the street where he collapsed and died. Kim Hai was shot while trying to subdue Fen Game. Ho Kai, who was ironing shirts in a back room, was shot at close range and died instantly. Fen Game put the gun in his pocket and headed for the Hop Wah Laundry on Casey Street where Hong Wing was working. Meanwhile, Ches Noseworthy, a resident of Carter's Hill, had contacted the police.

Fen Game barged into the Hop Wah laundry shouting Hong Wing's name. When wing appeared from a back room, Fen Game fired two shots. Wing was saved by a dipper he was holding which deflected the bullets, though one of them penetrated his shoulder. Fen Game went out into the street and fired a bullet into his own head. It failed to kill him. He was still standing as he unloaded the gun, put the bullets in his pocket and staggered down Barron Street, ending up at the Jim Gay Laundry on New Gower Street where he collapsed. As he was wheeled into the old General Hospital on Forest Road he muttered, "Me sin...me die tomorrow."

The bullet was successfully removed from Fen Game's head and after 16 days in hospital he was released and taken to prison. Meanwhile the three victims, to satisfy public interest in the crime, were placed on display in the windows of J.T. Martin Funeral Services on New Gower Street.

For Fen Game's trial, Justice officials sought an outside interpreter for the accused because it was felt the local Chinese community could not be trusted. Justice officials in Newfoundland may have hoped the accused would die, thereby saving the cost of a trial, as indicated in the letter sent to Ottawa requesting an interpreter. It read: "One of the members of the Chinese Community ran amuck and killed three of his countrymen and attempted to kill another and then unfortunately made an ineffectual attempt to commit suicide."

Fen Game confessed to the police at the hospital when he was expected to die, but this confession was later ruled inadmissable by the Court because the police had not given the suspect the police caution. However, the police investigation turned up a letter Fen Game had sent to his cousin in St. John's in which he confessed to all three killings.

Following a three month Magisterial Enquiry, the trial finally got underway on November 20. Representing the Crown was H.A. Winter while L.E.Emerson represented Wo Fen Game. The three presiding judges were Horwood, Johnson and Kent. The trail lasted six days with a total of 36 witnesses being called to testify.

An unusual scene took place during the trial when some of the Chinese witnesses were administered the oath in accordance with their Confucian beliefs. This required the witness to write his name on paper, set it on fire and hold it in his hand until it burned out.

Interest in the trial centered on whether or not the defence could show that the four shooting victims had conspired to kill Fen Game. Their argument was that Fen Game had shot the others in self-defence, knowing they were conspiring to kill him. The strength of the prosecution's case rested on two admissions of guilt made by Fen Game.

Although all Chinese witnesses denied that a feud existed the defence asked, "Why else would Fen Game seek out Hong Wing and not the others at the Hop Wah Laundry?" Emerson noted that if the dispute had simply been over loss of wages, Hong Wing would not have been a victim, as he was not party to that decision. Emerson also pointed to testimony that Kim Hi and Hong Loen had revolvers. The defence told the Court that Fen Game was a poor ignorant man which made it difficult to prepare a defence. The prosecution countered that Fen Game was not at all ignorant and pointed to the letters he had written from prison.

Fen Game feigned madness during the first days of the trial and the Chief Justice ordered that he be taken to the back of the court within hearing distance of the trial proceedings. A doctor administered shot of morphine to quieten him.

Fen Game's lawyer claimed he had shot the others in self-defence. But the law stated that a person assaulted is not justified in using firearms against his assailant unless he is in such a position as to make him consider his life is actually in danger.

Before the case went to jury the Chief Justice, after reviewing all evidence and the law, stated that there was, "strong evidence to show the murders were planned." He explained that "provocation sufficient to incite to kill must be gross if it is to result in the reducing of the charges to manslaughter. Nothing short of grave provocation is sufficient."

In conclusion the Justice asked the jury to discriminate between what is true and what is false. "Your duty is to declare the verdict according to the evidence and ours is to declare sentencing according to the verdict."

The jury took only one hour to reach its decision: guilty on all counts. The prisoner showed no reaction to the decision. He was escorted back to prison to await sentencing the next day.

That night Fen Game attempted to escape. He struck a guard with a brick and ran toward the main hall, where he was recaptured by guards. On November 25, Wo Fen Game was sentenced to be hanged.

At 7:45 am on Saturday, December 16, a large crowd gathered outside the penitentiary. A public notice of the hanging had been placed on the prison gate the night before. While the execution procession was preparing for the hanging inside the prison, the bell began to toll. Fen Game walked to the scaffold without faltering. He showed no emotion on his face as he stood on the trap door for nearly ten minutes. However, he shook and trembled when the executioner approached him.

The executioner fastened the rope around Fen Games neck. Reverend Fairbarn of Wesley Church stood on the corner of the scaffold reading the Services for the Dead while Reverend Joyce stood near the bottom, also praying. The executioner stepped back and pulled the lever releasing the bolts that held the trap door and Fen Game was launched into eternity. A black flag was hoisted over the prison to signify that the sentence of the Supreme Court had been carried out.

September 22, 1930
Tom Beckett Hanged

The bludgeoned body of a taxi driver discovered on a lonely Glace Bay road in Cape Breton set off an intensive police investigation and manhunt that spread to Newfoundland. On the evening of September 22nd, 1930, a Newfoundlander stepped into a Glace Bay taxi operated by Nicholas Mathos, known around Cape Breton as Nick the Greek. The passenger was 35-year-old George Alfred Beckett. Several hours later Mr. and Mrs. Andrew Lynch, walking along the deserted road, discovered the blood-spattered body of Mathos, who had been bludgeoned to death with an iron pipe.

The police were called to the scene and the investigation began. Meanwhile, George Beckett was visiting a girlfriend, Margaret Dupe. She recalled that he took a locket of her hair and forced open the back of a pocket watch to place the hair inside. This watch later played a key role in the trial of the murderer of Nick the Greek.

At the murder scene Detective Daniel Nicholas was piecing the puzzle together. He had determined that Nick was the victim of a robbery. A roll of small bills, some loose change and a pocket watch had been stolen. He also learned that the victim was last seen with George Beckett. While the investigation continued, Beckett returned to his home at Old Perlican, Nfld.

Detective Nicholas, meanwhile, had located a witness with a watch similar to the one stolen from Nick the Greek. When questioned, the man told police he had purchased it from George Beckett. The evidence was now strong enough for the police to obtain a warrant for the arrest of George

Alfred Beckett. Nicholas went to Old Perlican, arrested Beckett and returned him to Cape Breton where he was charged with murder. The trial got underway on February 19, 1931 amidst a raging snow storm. The storm did not dampen public interest and crowds filled the court room to watch the trail.

The Crown had no witness to the murder and relied on some convincing circumstantial evidence. The first witness was Tom Wall of Tompkins, Nfld. Wall identified the watch held as evidence by the Court as the one he purchased from Beckett. The owner of a jewellery store also identified the watch which he said was sold to the victim. He explained the watch had a private marking on it which showed ownership. Detective Nicholas told the Court, "The first time I had seen this time piece was at Tompkins, Nfld. where I found it in the possession of Tom Wall."

Next the Crown called restaurant owner A. Speers who testified that Nick the Greek had left his restaurant at around 6:25 pm and had shown him the watch just before leaving. The sequence of time was important to show that the murder happened when Beckett was with the Greek. John Byrne, a Glace Bay Power Plant worker told the Court that the whistle at the plant went off every night at 8:15pm. Mr. and Mrs. Lynch testified that they left their house to go for a walk just as the Plant whistle was sounding. They found the Greek's body 300 yards from their house. The Crown claimed that the murder occurred between 7 and 8 pm. . Another fact established by the prosecution was that Beckett had no money before the murder, and had plenty of money after the killing. The Crown rested its case.

With Beckett's life hanging in the balance and the defence summation his only hope to sway the jury, the crowds of spectators showed intense interest in every word uttered him. M.A. Patterson began, " Nobody had seen Beckett commit the crime. The Crown could prove him to have been no closer than two miles from the scene of the murder that night." He pointed out that many of the Crown witnesses were unreliable and charged the Crown with laxity in not summoning all available witnesses.

Patterson added: "The only evidence that Beckett was in Glace Bay on the night of the 22nd of September was that of [A. Speers] a rumseller, a thief, a man engaged in illegal business, and owner of an establishment where unlawful business was carried on" (a reference to shady dealings at Speers' restaurant). In respect to the watch evidence, Patterson said the Crown proved only that Nick the Greek owned the watch no later than June, 1930.He added,"When each individual circumstance is doubtful, therefore the whole claim of circumstances is doubtful. Circumstances can lie, as well as human beings. The life of this man rests solely with you and you should not find him guilty unless he is proven guilty beyond reasonable doubt."

Crown Prosecutor Neil McArthur responded to Patterson's summation. He said, "When officers of the Crown are engaged in the investigation of a crime they do not go to Sunday Schools for their information. They must resort to questionable places and must sometimes call witnesses who have committed offences against the law and have been in prison."

Justice Ross explained the law to the jury. He said, "The prisoner is presumed innocent until proven guilty beyond a reasonable doubt. The burden of proof rests with the Crown. There is no question of manslaughter in this case. The verdict must be either guilty or not guilty of murder. The Crown is relying upon a chain of circumstances which they hope to connect with the fact to be proven. It is most fortunate that we have such evidence, for murder is seldom witnessed. It is done usually under the cover of darkness. The Crown is not asking that you convict on one circumstance alone, they ask for a conviction on the whole chain of evidence laid before you."

The jury deliberated for one and a half hours and returned a guilty verdict. When asked if he had anything to say, Beckett, responded, "I have nothing to say." Justice Ross then proceeded to sentence Beckett to be hanged on April 30, 1931. While walking from the Court, Beckett commented to spectators, "Tough luck."

At 1:10 am Newfoundland time on Thursday, April 30, 1931, Beckett was taken from his cell to the gallows at the Cape Breton Prison. When the Warden arrived to take him to the gallows Beckett was composed but knelt in prayer beside his bed. He remained very calm as the procession moved towards the gallows.

The hooded executioner, a little shorter than Beckett, reached up to place the rope around his neck, then stepped back to await the warden's instructions. Beckett remained motionless as the warden nodded and the platform beneath Beckett opened. The rope quivered for a minute or so then stopped. Thirteen minutes later he was cut down and certified dead by the prison doctor.

After the execution a ballad made its way around Newfoundland which was claimed to have been written by Beckett while he awaited execution. It was called "The Ballad of George Alfred Beckett" and was sung to the music of "The Wild Colonial Boy." (Convicted, Jesperson Press, Fitzgerald, 1983).

December 31, 1930
New Year's Eve Murder
at Corner Brook

An Ivor Johnson revolver was used to fire a bullet from close range into the skull of John Thistle at his home at Curling on Newfoundland's West Coast. The murder sparked three separate trials and attracted a great deal of public attention.

Thistle was shot through the back of his head on New Year's Eve,1930. Only two other people were in the house that night: Thistle's attractive 26 year old wife Rita, and her suspected lover, 23 year old Reginald Boland. The police investigation that followed was full of twists and surprises. Rita Thistle gave three separate stories to investigators before the police eventually made an arrest.

Police Sergeant Peter Lee became suspicious at the hospital while Doctors struggled to same the victim's life. He noticed that Thistle's hands were covered in coal dust. Soon after Thistle died, Lee investigated the scene of the shooting. Rita Thistle had scrubbed the floors, removing all evidence of blood stains and whatever else might be found. However, Lee found a gun in the pantry off the kitchen. Three shots had been fired but only one bullet was accounted for. That bullet was lodged in the brain of John Thistle. When Rita claimed her husband had committed suicide, Lee concealed his disbelief.

While Lee questioned neighbours, Rita called him back to her home and confessed that she had lied. She then claimed that Reg Boland had shot her husband. The 23 year old Boland had visited her often while her husband worked at his barber shop. He usually escaped detection by leaving the house through the cellar and out the hatch on the side of the home.

However, on the night of the murder someone had locked the hatch and when Boland attempted his usual escape he found himself trapped in the cellar. Rita wanted to make sure that Boland had left the cellar and she volunteered to go there to get coal. But her husband grabbed the coal bucket and said he would do it. When he got down into the cellar , she heard him say, "What are you doing there?"

Rita told police that the two men came up into the kitchen. She became frightened and went to the pantry. She said she saw Boland pull a gun and shoot her husband. He then told her to get a bottle and hit him over the head with it. She told police later that Boland had sent her a note while John was waking, asking her to keep quiet and to burn the note after reading it.

This conversation with Rita Thistle heightened Lee's suspicions. Two bullets were still unaccounted for, and he noted in the pantry that 22 bottles were neatly arranged and not one was out of place. Nor was there any sign of a struggle in the kitchen area.

The next morning, Lee arrested Boland at his home. Boland denied owning a gun and insisted he had no romantic involvement with Rita Thistle.

Meanwhile, Rita Thistle changed her story again and told police that her husband had struggled with Boland over the gun and she tried but was unable to break it up.

The trial took place in St. John's on February 23, 1931. The prosecutor, F. Gordon Bradley, relied on his key witness, Rita Thistle. She testified that she saw the accused pull the gun and scuffle with her husband. The gun went off and Boland fled the scene.

Defence lawyer Jim Higgins called Reg Boland, who gave

a different version of what took place. Boland claimed he was
innocently visiting Mrs. Thistle, and went to the cellar to get
away when he heard Jack return. He said he thought Jack
would be mad at him for visiting Rita while Jack was not
home. He said that Jack caught him in the cellar, they both
came up into the kitchen, and Boland said he ran from the
house. A half hour later he returned to the neighbourhood to
visit a friend and heard screams and several shots fired. Only
the next morning did he learn of Thistle's death. He admitted
he sent a letter to Rita, but not to ask her to keep quiet. He
recalled that he was offering her help if needed.

Medical evidence at trial showed that the death could not
have been caused by suicide. The jury took less than an hour
to return a "Not Guilty" verdict for Reg Boland. But a week
later, the case took a sensational twist when Rita Thistle was
arrested and charged with the murder. The roles of Rita and
Boland were now reversed; she became the accused, and he
the crown witness.

The evidence presented at trial was similar to the first
trial. This time the prosecution argued that Boland should be
believed. With no other direct evidence on who killed Thistle,
the case came down to the question of who to believe, Thistle
or Boland. Boland testified he left Jack and Rita Thistle alone
in the house. Suicide was ruled out, so Rita had to be the
killer. The jury were out for an hour and ten minutes and
returned a verdict of "Not Guilty" for Rita Thistle.

Had the real murderer gotten away scot free with one of
the most serious offenses in our Criminal Code? Possibly not!
Rita Thistle's trial showed that Boland perjured himself four
times during the two trials. If Boland was the murderer, he
didn't escape justice completely. He was re-arrested and
indicted by the Grand Jury on four counts of perjury.

While Boland pleaded not guilty, the jury did not agree.

He was found guilty and sentenced to five years at Her Majesty's Penitentiary. The judge commented, "We don't know what the outcome of your trial would have been if you had told the truth during your first trial."

January 25, 1931

Rum Runners

A U.S. Coast Guard cutter pulled up to within thirty feet of the schooner *Josephine K*, which was under the command of a Newfoundland skipper named William Cluett. Without any warning, the Coast Guard cutter opened fire on the slow-moving vessel. The first bullet went across the bow while the second crashed through the wheelhouse and penetrated Captain Cluett's chest. Cluett fell out the wheelhouse door as his ship came to a stop. This incident took place on January 25, 1931.

In minutes the Coast Guard crew, with rifles and guns loaded and ready to fire, stormed the *Josephine K*. The fifteen-man crew, which included four Newfoundlanders, was placed under arrest and taken aboard the cutter to New York City. The incident attracted worldwide attention and for a short while it seemed as if an international diplomatic confrontation would occur.

It was the era of Al Capone, and prohibition was making rum-running a profitable but dangerous business. The Cluett brothers of St. John's were experienced and respected seamen. Bill was captain of the *Josephine K*, which was owned by the Liverpool Shipping Company and registered at Digby, Nova Scotia. His brother Alf was chief engineer on the vessel.

The brothers were attracted to the rumrunning trade by the high profits, danger and excitement. Not only were they at constant risk of being caught by the Coast Guard, but they were competing with U.S. gangsters who were bent on monopolizing the rum-running business. One gangster syndicate operating in the New England states had over thirty-seven boats as part of their operation.

These criminals took great pains to stay outside the twelve-mile limit. They usually transferred their cargoes to other vessels outside the limit. It was difficult to capture them because of their expensive, sophisticated communications systems.

A Coast Guard spokesman explained, "When arrests were made, it was unusual to find any money on board, or on the skipper or crew....The financial exchanges were made on shore [which] made authorities' work a lot more difficult."

When the captured crewmen of the *Josephine K* arrived in New York, Captain Cluett was immediately rushed to a hospital, where he died shortly afterwards. The other crewmembers were charged in court with rumrunning and confined to jail. Alfred Cluett however, was let out on bail by the New York judge in order to attend his brother's funeral.

The victim was twenty-eight years old and had lived in Lunenburg, Nova Scotia with his wife and five year old son. Members of the Cluett family from Newfoundland travelled to Lunenburg to attend the funeral. The people of Lunenburg were outraged over the tragedy and for the first time in 178 years a funeral sermon was preached in St. John's Anglian Church. Reverend E. Ryder described the death of Cluett as one of the inevitable tragedies that followed the hypocrisy of prohibition. He told those attending that Cluett's death was "nothing more than murder on the high seas." The clergyman paid tribute to Captain Cluett, describing him as "a good husband and father."

The incident captured world-wide attention, and both the Dominion government of Newfoundland and the Canadian Government expressed grave concern over the killing. They demanded an investigation, claiming that the incident took place near Ambrose Lighthouse, southeast of Rockaway, Long Island and outside the twelve-mile limit. The American government responded by ordering an immediate investigation into the incident.

Following the funeral, Alf Cluett visited his mother, who operated a hotel on Water Street in St. John's. Alf, a debonair, handsome, witty and intelligent seaman, was interviewed by an Evening Telegram reporter. He told the reporter that the incident with the Americans was the first confrontation with authorities in his five years of rumrunning. "The *Josephine K* was well outside the twelve-mile limit when the U.S. cutter ran up to within thirty feet and fired several shots without giving the least signal or warning. The second shot went into the wheelhouse, hitting my brother. Bill immediately ordered the engines stopped and then he fell out through the wheelhouse door. The coast-guard crew were under the influence of liquor at the time."

Alf was bitter over the Coast Guard's refusal to permit him to speak with his dying brother. He told the Telegram,, "I was the last to see him alive before they took him to a hospital at Staten Island."

Alf indicated he intended to return to the rumrunning trade, explaining that he loved the salt water and the excitement connected to this risky undertaking. His mother told the reporter she was proud of her son but she wanted him to quit the rumrunning business. Alf said he loved the business because there was plenty to eat and drink and lots of money in it. The Cluetts' cargo consisted of liquor with an estimated value of $100,000.

Meanwhile, the American inquiry completely exonerated the Coast Guard from any blame. It also upheld the action of the cutter in firing on the *Josephine K*. The report determined that the vessel was ten miles off the U.S. coast and was in the process of transferring its illegal cargo to an American vessel named the Brooklyn. It also found that Cluett was accidentally shot while the Coast Guard were effecting a legal arrest.

Cluett and his crew were convicted and given a heavy fine. Whether he returned to rum-running, as he promised, is not known.

July, 1935

Newfoundland Rangers

Prior to Confederation in 1949, two police forces maintained the peace throughout Newfoundland and Labrador. The Newfoundland Constabulary under the Department of Justice policed the Avalon and Bonavista peninsulas, while the Newfoundland Rangers policed all other parts of the province. They were the responsibility of the Department of Natural Resources.

The famous Newfoundland Ranger Force came into being during Commission of Government. The Force began during July, 1935 under Sir John Hope Simpson, the first commissioner for natural Resources. The first commanding officer was Major Len Stick, who was a veteran of World War I and had served with the royal Newfoundland Regiment at Gallipoli and Beaumont Hamel.

The Newfoundland Government arranged with the Canadian Government for RCMP Sergeant T. Anderson to come to Newfoundland and conduct a six-week training course for the Ranger recruits.

The Ranger Force started with an enrolment of thirty men and two officers. Originally they were headquartered at Whitbourne but later they moved their headquarters to Kilbride. For a dollar a day, "Newfoundland's finest" were expected to risk their lives in all sorts of weather, arrest lunatic murderers, deliver babies and help citizens complete government forms.

The Ranger Force wore a distinctive uniform. It consisted of a khaki tunic and breeches with a brown stripe down the side, high leather boots and a military-style peaked cap. On the hat was a badge showing a caribou's head with the one word motto of the Force, "Ubique," meaning "everywhere."

These men really lived up to the motto. They travelled across some of Newfoundland's toughest terrain, in boats, with dog teams, on horses and on foot. One did not require a driver's licence to become a ranger. However, a ranger stationed at Clarenville was issued a motorcycle. Empowered to test others for licensing, the ranger tested himself and earned his cycle licence.

The first casualty in the Force occurred during the winter of 1938 when Ranger Danny Corcoran, stationed at Harbour Deep, was lost while on patrol. He was found two weeks later, but died at the hospital in St. Anthony. In 1939 Ranger Mike Green and his horse fell through the ice while on a patrol near Lamaline. He struggled to land, but died of exposure.

The Ranger Force was disbanded on July 31, 1950 with most of the Rangers joining the RCMP.

January 5, 1936
Lake Family Murdered

What first appeared to be the accidental death of three people in a house fire developed into one of the most bizarre criminal cases in the history of Atlantic Canada. The "Baby Doll Murder," as the case was dubbed, took place at Pacific Junction near Dorchester, New Brunswick on Sunday, January 5, 1936. The victims were Newfoundlanders: Phil Lake, his wife Bertha and their 20 month old son Jack.

On Monday, January 6, family friend Otto Blakeney left his job in the woods to have lunch with the Lake's. From a distance he could see the Lake cabin in smouldering ruins. He ran to the site in hopes of finding survivors but was horrified to discover the body of Phil Lake, whose arms and legs had been burned completely off in the fire.

Blakeney ran along the railway tracks towards the CN offices for help and along the way came across the bodies of 20 month old Jackie Lake and his mother Bertha, who was partially clothed. There were blood stains in the area and the baby's bottle was covered in blood. The RCMP were called in and an investigation started. Still unaccounted for was the Lake's infant child Betty.

While Bertha's body was being removed, Sgt. Bedford Peters noted two sets of tracks in the snow. The police followed the tracks, and noting the small holes in the snow alongside each track, suspected they had been left by a cane. Bedford picked up a glove which he believed someone had dropped in a rush to get away. It turned out to be a valuable piece of evidence which helped the RCMP solve the murder.

CNR employee David Barron gave police another piece

of the puzzle. He recalled that at dusk the previous day, he had seen one of the Bannisters, a family who lived nearby, walking along the tracks near the Lake home. Police went to the Bannister home and were met at the door by Danny Bannister. Danny, known in the community as a dim-wit, saw the glove in the police officer's hand and before any questions were asked stated, "Hey, that's mine, where'd you guys get that?" He said he had loaned his gloves to his brother Art but they had not been returned. Barron identified Art as the man he seen near the Lake home. The RCMP arrested Art Bannister and he quickly confessed to the killings.

He confessed that he often dropped in to visit his friends the Lakes. On the day of the tragedy he was there when his sister Francis and brother Danny came in. Art claimed that Phil Lake made a pass at Frances which sparked a fight between Lake and the Bannister brothers. He said, "Phil threw a small fire log which accidentally struck his wife on the head. Danny then picked up a piece of board and hit Phil Lake on the head. An oil-lamp was tipped over during the scuffle and the place caught fire." Danny and Frances told similar stories to police. Danny was arrested and Frances became a Crown witness.

The case then took a bizarre twist. Milton Trites, a neighbour of the Bannister's, informed police that there was a baby at the home of Ma Bannister, mother of the trio. The RCMP searched Ma Bannister's house against her objections and found an infant child which they identified as Betty Lake, whom they had believed was cremated in the fire.

Further police investigation disclosed that Ma had been perpetrating a charade for months using a doll. Many neighbours told police of seeing Ma carrying a bundle in her arms, which all assumed was a baby. The answer to the mystery came from Milton Trites. A year before the murders, Ma had worked as a housekeeper for the Trites. She thought Trites had money and she developed a plan to extort money from him. In November 1935 she quit her job telling Trites she was pregnant and that he was responsible. A day after the Lakes were found, Ma invited Trites to her home and showed him the baby, which she claimed was his.

Her blackmail scheme wasn't limited to Trites. The second victim was to be Albert Powell, a Sunday School teacher. Ma accused Powell of getting her daughter Marie pregnant and planned to pass the Lake baby off as Powell's baby, also.

Frances Bannister was a good witness for the Crown. She contradicted her brothers' story that Lake made a pass at her. She testified that she remained outside the house when her two brothers went inside. She said that Art passed out the baby and she began to walk home. She heard a scream from inside but kept walking. Her brothers caught up with her and they walked along together.

Responding to claims that Phil had been a tall, powerful man who could not have been overpowered by the young Bannisters, the RCMP ordered his body to be exhumed. The coroner's examination showed that Lake had been shot with a .22 calibre bullet which lodged in his brain. The RCMP then presented the possibility that the marks in the snow along the track which they had suspected were cane marks, were actually caused by a rifle. Police scoured the area and found the murder weapon, which belonged to Art Bannister.

On March 10, 1936 the Crown ended its case and the defence chose not to call any witnesses.

Both Daniel and Arthur Bannister were found guilty of murder and sentenced to hang. The executions took place at the county jail in Dorchester, on September 23, 1936. Ma Bannister, who masterminded the kidnapping and extortion plot, was found guilty of harbouring a stolen child. She was sentenced to three and a half years in prison. After being released Ma returned to live at her home near Dorchester, where she died in 1971.

July 3, 1938

The Bizarre Water St. Cafe Killing

On the morning of July 3, 1938, Kilbride farmer Gordon Stanley found the body of Eng Wing Kit hanging from an iron bar in the kitchen of the Regal Cafe, Water Street West, St. John's. The finding set into motion an intensive investigation by the CID which saw every member of the Chinese community in St. John's interrogated and which finally led to the arrest of Quang John Shang of Duckworth Street.

Wing Kit, known to local residents as "Charlie," was found hanging from a piece of iron pipe which had been laid from the kitchen table to the stove. He had been strangled. A knife had penetrated his voice box and his throat had been slashed. A flour sack had been folded and tied around the neck with twine, obviously to prevent bleeding. A circular piece of flesh had been cut from the chest and there were large bruises on the chest and upper left arm. The murderer had then tied three bands of rope around the neck, raising the victim's head about a foot from the floor, and tied the rope tightly to the iron pipe. Several segments of the rope had been carefully fashioned in a figure eight. Charlie, dressed in pyjamas and apron, was covered in blood with his purple tongue extending from his mouth.

Stanley ran from the Cafe to get help. He caught up with

Constable Spracklin as he was about to board the street car. Within an hour the place was crawling with police. Physical evidence and blood samples were gathered and sent to the Pathology Department of Dalhousie University for examination. Police investigators then began an intensive effort to question all members of the Chinese community in St. John's. They started with the five Chinese laundry men living next door to the Regal Cafe. Three of the five laundrymen were at home at the time of the murder and although they denied any knowledge of the murder, police suspected they knew something. Police notes claimed it was easy for the laundry occupants to hear any conversation or quarrelling at the Regal because of the thin walls separating the two establishments.

The leaders of the Chinese community assisted police by encouraging possible witnesses to come forward. They offered support and protection to anyone with information to help investigators. The effort paid off. Two men from the West End Laundry, Tom Soon and Tom Loon, came forward with information which lead to the arrest of Quang John Shang.

Tom Soon said he saw and heard Shang inside the Regal on the night of the murder. Tom Loon claimed he saw Shang walking up Leslie Street away from the Regal shortly after the time the murder was alleged to have occurred. On Tuesday night, July 12, 1938, Shang was arrested as he was leaving the Holland Cafe on New Gower Street. It was Shang's tenth anniversary in Newfoundland, having arrived here on July 12, 1928.

Following the preliminary enquiry Shang was committed to stand trial on October 31, 1938. The crown was represented by L. Emerson and G.B. Summers. Shang was represented by C.J. Fox and James Power. Gordon Yuen of the

Canadian Department of Justice was sworn in as interpreter for the trial.

Tom Soon testified that a few minutes after he went to bed he heard arguing coming from the Regal Cafe. He said he got out of bed, dressed and went into the rear garden where he peeked into the Regal's kitchen window. He said he saw Quang John Shang and heard him say, "I am going to have some bread." Soon said he then went back to bed. However, he again heard loud noises and something being dragged across the floor. He got dressed and again went to peek through the Regal window. He said he saw Shang but did not see the victim. When he returned to his bed room he heard footsteps next door, followed by someone leaving the place.

Tom Loon then testified that he saw Shang at about 1 a.m., walking up Leslie Street near the Regal Cafe. Loon had taken an ABC Cab on a message to York Street at 11:30 p.m. and was returning home in the cab at the time of the sighting.

Defence lawyer Fox cast doubt on Loon's testimony by calling Ambrose Harris, the cab driver, as witness. Harris testified that he drove Loon home that night but he did not see anyone on Leslie Street or near the Regal Cafe.

Fox attacked the credibility of the two key prosecution witnesses and in doing so cast suspicion on them. He told the jury it was strange that when police went to the laundry the morning of the murder they found a big fire in the kitchen of the laundry. The laundry was not opened and they had stopped working at 4 pm the day before. "Were they burning something?" he asked the jury. He added that the same night Soon and Loon were out in the garden behind the Regal cutting and removing weeds "Why?" He continued, "The two men explained they were nervous and feared the spirit of the victim. Cutting the weeds, they claimed, would keep the spirit away. Tom Yuen, an occupant of the laundry, was so nervous that night that he slept with two other Chinamen. Why was he so nervous?" Fox suggested that Eng Wing Kit may have been killed elsewhere.

Fox concluded saying: "The Crown had not produced one bit of substantiated evidence to convict the accused. God's greatest gift to man is life and the life of the accused is now in the hands of the jury. I am not appealing to your sympathies but to your sense of British Justice."

Emerson summed up the Crown's case. He stated that the two witnesses had seen Shang inside and near the cafe at the estimated time of the murder. He added, "It is not the Crown's duty to overstate the case against the accused. It is my duty to bring before you the direct evidence against the accused. You have heard the evidence. You have the final word. My learned friend referred to circumstantial evidence. If the courts waited for complete evidence there would be many criminals abroad today."

The Judge reviewed the evidence presented and stated, "It is not for the accused to establish his innocence but for the Crown to establish his guilt. In civil cases the preponderance of probability may constitute sufficient grounds for a guilty verdict, but something more in the way of proof is required in criminal cases. In order to return a verdict against the prisoner you must be satisfied beyond a reasonable doubt of his guilt. If you think the Crown's case is conclusive it is your duty to pronounce the prisoner guilty. But if you feel the case has left you in doubt, so that you cannot safely convict, you will remember that it is better that many guilty men should escape than that one innocent man should be wrongly convicted."

After a four and a half hour deliberation the jury returned its "Not guilty" verdict to a crowded courtroom. The prisoner showed no emotion when the Court interpreter told him he was a free man. Shang was escorted from the courthouse by friends, including Kim Lee, the leader of the Chinese community in St. John's. For years after people in the neighbourhood speculated that the two crown witnesses, Tom Soon and Tom Loon, were the real killers. However, police had no evidence connecting the two to the crime.

The murder of Eng Wing Kit remains among Newfoundland's many unsolved mysteries.

December 25, 1942

Water Street Riot

On the evening of Christmas Day, December 25, 1942, the Chinese owners of the Imperial Cafe, located on the north side of Water Street near the intersection of Prescott Street, were entertaining some friends in their restaurant. The Imperial, like all other city businesses, was closed to the public that Christmas Day. Three sailors from a British naval vessel tied up at the St. John's Harbour had walked the whole length of Water Street looking for an open restaurant, club or store, but without success.

As they neared the Prescott Street intersection, they noticed the Imperial Cafe was lit up and appeared to be doing business. However, when they tried to enter through the front door, they discovered it was locked. One of the seaman knocked on the door, but the manager, visible through the window, raised his hand and shook his head to indicate the restaurant was closed. This angered the sailors, who perhaps misunderstood the manager's hand signals.

One of the men took a step back, raised his foot and

delivered a swift, hard kick to the door which sent it swinging wide open. Several Chinese men attending the party rushed to the aid of the owner. During the ensuing struggle, which spilled over into Water Street, the sailors took a beating from the Chinese. One of the sailors was struck on the head with a bottle which almost knocked him unconscious. Defeated, the trio left the Imperial and returned to their ship. The Chinese made temporary repairs to the broken door and continued on with their celebrations.

Meanwhile, the three sailors spread the word among their shipmates of the beating they had received from a group of Chinese. The crewmembers felt the beating was an insult to the British Navy, and almost to a man they began to leave the ship and head towards the Imperial. In a matter of minutes a full ship's company of 150 sailors was marching down Water Street to avenge their honour.

A Chinese guest at the Restaurant was distracted by a commotion outside. He went to the window to see what was happening and was startled to see a horde of English sailors approaching the front door of the Cafe. He shouted to his friends in the Cafe and they began running for safety. Some ran out the back door; others hid upstairs.

The sailors kicked in the front door and proceeded to wreck the restaurant. They beat out glass windows, broke the door off hinges and tossed furniture out into Water Street. Grabbing whatever food was available, and emptying the fridges the men painted the walls and ceiling with rice, coconut pie, lemon pie, catsup and sugar. They poured soup over the floor and emptied a bag of flour on top of it.

It took a combination of local police and the Navy Patrol to disperse the rioters. When they left, the cafe was in shambles. Police warned the Chinese community to remain inside until things settled down. The matter eventually settled down and there was no further trouble. The British sailors felt they had succeeded in getting revenge for the beating they had taken.

October 23, 1949

Alfred Beaton

Nineteen-year-old Alfred Beaton of Norris Arm spent the afternoon of October 23, 1949, drinking home brew and joking with friends. But later that night he met his ex-girl-friend, Margaret Stuckless, at a local club. That was when Beaton became unhinged. Margaret was sitting with another ex-boy friend, Jim Dwyer, and Ruby Elliott. Beaton insisted that she leave with him. Outside, he asked, "Who do you want, me or Jim?. She thought he was joking and answered, "Either one of you will do."

Margaret walked away. Beaton followed and close be-hind him was Jim Dwyer. Jim heard Margaret scream and say, "I've been stabbed." He recalled, "I then felt a blow on the head and felt dizzy. When I came to there was nobody around." Several friends inside the club had come out and taken Margaret to Mrs. Budgell's for assistance.

Jim Dwyer went home. As he walked up the steps of his house Beaton came out of the darkness and said, "You ran, didn't you? I'll get you." Jim went inside and locked the door. Beaton fired several shots into the house and left. Only property damage occurred.

Beaton's aunt Johanna Manuel heard the shooting and came out to see what was happening. She shouted, "Who fired that shot?" Beaton replied, "I did." Johanna said, "Alf, my son, do you know you are not allowed to have that gun out tonight?" He didn't answer. She moved towards him saying, "Give me the gun and you can have it in the morning." Beaton held the gun tightly and answered with a determined, "No," adding as he looked up towards the sky,"Do you see that there in the sky, I've got to have all that tonight before I'm finished." He turned away and as he left he commented, "Don't shed any tears for me tonight." Johanna was confused. As she walked back to the house, she heard more shooting.

Meanwhile, Margaret's mother and Dot Manuel had heard about the stabbing and gone to Budgell's to help out. The girl had been stabbed near the left eye. Mrs. Budgell cleaned and bandaged the wound. Satisfied that margaret was all right, Mrs. Stuckless and Dot left.

They certainly picked the wrong time to go outside because Beaton was lurking in the darkness nearby. He was in a rage and determined to hurt more people. He began his shooting spree by firing in the darkness at the two women. A bullet hit and killed Dot Manuel.

His fifteen-year-old cousin Leonard had a brush with death when Alfred fired at him. The bullet passed through Leonard's windbreaker and shirt without touching his body. Leonard rushed home and herded his mother and two brothers into a punt to row to a neighbour's where his father was playing cards. He wanted to avoid the dangers on the dark road at Norris Arm where Beaton was indiscriminately firing his gun.

Beaton next fired at Sam Elliott, who retreated to his house and barricaded himself inside. While the community took refuge, Newfoundland Ranger Bruce Gillingham and Margaret Stuckless's brothers Jack and Norman armed themselves and set out to put a stop to Beaton's shooting spree.

They caught up with Beaton and before he could swing his gun towards them, Gillingham jumped over a wire fence and tackled him to the ground. Beaton was hand cuffed and taken to Botwood. Before leaving Norris Arm, he asked Jack to tell Margaret that he was sorry for what he did. Gillingham recalled, "Beaton was like a man angry about something."

At Botwood, Alf Beaton confessed to the shootings. he was taken to St. John's and charged with murder, which carried the death penalty.

The jury deliberated for an hour and forty-five minutes and returned a guilty verdict. Justice Emerson asked Beaton if he had anything to say, to which he replied by shaking his head "No." When Emerson pronounced the death sentence, Beaton's face flushed, but his expression didn't change.

Two policemen escorted Beaton, who looked straight ahead as he left the court chambers. Outside, however, he drew his handkerchief and broke down crying. There was no recommendation for mercy.

On February 11, 1950, the Justice Department issued a press statement announcing that the Governor, after consulting with his Commissioners, had decided to commute the death penalty to life imprisonment, with a provision that there be a parole review in ten years and periods not exceeding three years thereafter. Beaton was eventually released on parole. Alfred Beaton was the last Newfoundlander tried for capital murder prior to Newfoundland becoming a province of Canada. Less than sixty days after the end of his trial, Newfoundland became Canada's tenth province.

Chapter Five

Later Twentieth Century

January, 1950

Murder at Gander

Sixteen year old George Dwyer had had a troubled upbringing. He was born at Norris Arm on December 24, 1933. His mother passed away when he was three years old and his sister Agnes cared for him after that. After George finished grade seven he moved to live with another sister, Philomena, and her husband Pat Burke at Gander.

George dropped out of school and found himself a job with John Higden, who paid him thirty dollars a month and some extra money whenever he worked on Sunday. George got along well with his brother-in-law Pat, but paid no board. Instead he purchased clothing and toys for the Burke children. There was no dispute over the payment of board until just before Christmas in 1949 when his sister told him he would have to start paying board. George wasn't happy with the request and felt it was prompted by Pat Burke.

At the same time, the bicycle used by George became an issue. Burke, who worked at the fire hall, owned the bicycle.

Burke offered to sell it to George for five dollars. George didn't have the money but offered to pay for it when he got paid. At this point he believed the bicycle belonged to him.

One day George returned home, leaving the bike at his place of work. His sister scolded him for not bringing it home. He left the house in an angry mood and went to the fire hall where Pat worked. Ordinarily George got along well with his brother-in-law and often dropped in at the fire hall to visit or borrow books.

On this occasion, however, Pat Burke was angry and shouted at George in front of other firemen. He said, "If you don't get the bike back from the last place you left it, you, not the bike, will be outside." George later told police, "Pat made a proper show of me in front of the men." George brooded over the incident all night and was upset even more the next morning when Pat went to cut wood without asking him to come along. He usually took George, but this time he invited George Dawe and Clarence Price.

The family rift bothered George all that day. At 4 p.m. he went to Tucker's Store at Gander where he purchased a gun, five boxes of shells containing fifty shells and a knife. When the clerk asked him why he was buying so many shells he replied, "For target practice." On his way to the Lion's Club shooting range he met a friend, Frank Ireland, and sent him to the store to buy an orange and some biscuits.

When Ireland returned, George took the food, and climbed into the window of the fire hall at the airport, where he ate the lunch and smoked a few cigarettes. At about 5:50 p.m. he saw Pat and his friends passing hangar 14 as they walked out of the woods towards where he was hiding.

George later told police he knew Pat would take the short cut but insisted he did not purchase the gun to kill him. However, when Pat came in view George thought he would give him a good fright by firing at him. Recalling the incident he said, "I took a pot shot at Pat just to frighten or wound him. I didn't care which."

When Pat passed where George was hiding George moved out and fired the gun at him. Pat was hit and fell to the ground. His friends got him into a taxi and rushed him to the Banting Memorial Hospital where he passed away shortly after arrival.

Meanwhile, George had removed the empty shells from his gun and went to the police station, where he reported the incident. He was arrested and charged with murder. The two-day trial ended on March 31. At 9 p.m. the jury returned its guilty verdict with a strong recommendation for mercy. Mercy was shown, and George Dwyer was given life imprisonment rather than the death sentence.

June 16, 1950
Mary Allen Strangled

Mary Allen left her mother's home at 16 Stephen Street near midnight on June 16, 1950, accompanied by a male friend. As she left, her mother, Jane Allen, warned her not to be long. Jane never saw her daughter alive again. When Mary failed to return home that night her mother became concerned. She did not report her daughter missing to the police but she did question neighbours and friends. Word of Mary's disappearance spread around town.

Meanwhile, Stan Butt of 129 Gower Street had become suspicious. The tenants renting from him on the first flat had not been seen for days and there was a foul odour coming from the room. His son Gordon contacted the Constabulary and Constable Austin Hann was sent to investigate.

After speaking with Stan Butt, Constable Hann attempted to enter the room, but the door was locked. He waited for the arrival of Inspector Mike Cahill, who used a skeleton key to gain entry. They were sickened by the dreadful odour. At first the room seemed empty and nothing out of place. Then Hann noticed a hand sticking out from beneath the bed. The two policemen lifted the bed and found Mary Allen. The victim wore a coat but was nude inside.She had been beaten and strangled. Cahill sent for the Chief of Police.

A warrant was issued for the arrest of the tenant, Walter Sweeney. A police alert was sent across the province describing Sweeney. Constable Jim Carter at Conception Harbour received a report that Sweeney was driving his way in a truck. Carter intercepted the truck, which was occupied by Sweeney and his wife.

Sweeney was arrested and taken to St. John's. His wife was brought to her mother's home at Signal Hill. A rumour spread around town that the girl had been strangled to cover up a pregnancy. Although this rumour continued for decades, medical evidence showed that the victim was not pregnant. The medical examiner determined that Mary Allen had died as the result of strangulation. The beating was not severe enough to cause death, he said.

Walter Sweeney gave police a statement. He said, "When I woke up in the morning I was on my back. I looked up at the ceiling before I looked anywhere else. I put my feet over the bed. I had all my clothes on except my coat. I almost put my feet on one of her arms or something. Whatever it was I fell back on the bed almost dead. A few seconds later I looked down on the floor and saw her there. I was worried. I did not know what happened." The sight of the slain victim upset

Sweeney and he grabbed a bottle of liquor from the table and took a drink. He than sank onto a chair. He recalled, "Then I was looking at her and all around, then I said to myself I must have done it, or there must have been someone else here with me. I think I must have been imagining to myself that there must have been someone else there."

Sweeney recalled events of the night of the killing. After picking up his pay as a longshore worker, he met a friend, Bill Parsley. The two picked up two girls and went to Jerry Byrne's Tavern on Topsail Road and then the tavern at the Octagon. They were back in town by 10:30 p.m. and went their separate ways.

Taxi driver Ed White recalled picking Mary Allen up on Queen Street with a young male friend and driving her to her mother's house on Stephen Street. She invited him into the house for a drink. He accepted. White told police that there was a man in the house whom he identified as Walter Sweeney. He said when he changed twenty dollars for Sweeney he noticed he had a bottle of rum in his belt. He said he then drove Walter Sweeney, Mary Allen, and the eighteen year old young man to 129 Gower St. Mary gave the young man twenty-five cents and he returned to Queen Street.

White told the police that Mary didn't like the look of the place on Gower Street and refused to leave the car. Sweeney coaxed her and she finally agreed. However, she warned him that if she didn't like the place she would leave. Sweeney's story was similar to White's.

Sweeney noted that next morning at 7:30 a.m. his brother-in-law Willis Chislett arrived. He didn't tell him right away. They both went out for breakfast and when they returned he showed Chislett the body and insisted he had nothing to do with the death. He said the girl and his buddy Bill Parsley were drinking when Sweeney went to sleep. He awoke in the middle of the night and saw the girl strike Parsley. He added that his friend struck the girl and she fell backwards, striking her head on the bed and stove as she hit the floor.

Sweeney added that when he awoke in the morning Parsley was gone and Mary Allen was dead on the floor. He put her under the bed and he tossed her clothing over her. When Chislett suggested he call the police, he refused. He commented, "I didn't do it. Let the ones that did it come and take her out of it." He then said he would get his buddies and a car to dump the body somewhere. Chislett refused to help. Chislett claimed that while he was there, Bill Parsley and Walter's brother Ron came into the room. Parsley admitted to being there but said Ron Sweeney was not there at the time. He told police he did not see the body.

The trial started October 24, 1950. Jim Higgins defended Sweeney. Harry Carter acted for the Crown and Sir Albert Walsh was the presiding judge. Several witnesses were called on the first day. Jane Allen, Mary's mother, described the last time she saw her daughter alive. She said Mary left her house at midnight with Sweeney and said she would not be home that night. Others living at 129 Gower Street testified they heard nothing out of the usual that night.

Higgins attempted to raise doubts about his client's guilt when he called Joan Furlong to the stand. Furlong lived at 118 Gower Street. She told the court that near 1 a.m. she saw Mary Allen arguing with an American soldier on Gower Street. Furlong's husband then called for her to come inside and she did. She testified she did not know anything about what happened afterwards.

Pathologist Dr. Ed Josephson, testified that death was caused by strangulation. He also gave details of injuries involved in a beating and noted that he found blood on the walls as high as forty-five inches.

Sweeney did not take the stand. However, in his statement to police he said he picked up his wife on Monday and brought her to the room. He then showed her the body and insisted he had no knowledge of what had happened. Higgins told the court that Sweeney did not take the stand because everything in his statement was the truth. He added that his client had ample to time to change his statement but he did not. Higgins suggested that the use of strangulation was alien to the average Newfoundlander, a statement believed to have been aimed at casting suspicion on an unidentified American serviceman. He told the jury there were grave doubts as to his client's guilt and called upon them to acquit Walter Sweeney.

Carter told the jury that they could reduce the charge to manslaughter if they felt Sweeney was too drunk to have sufficient control of his faculties. The judge instructed the jury that the questions they should consider were; "Did the accused kill Mary Allen? Did he intend to kill her or strangle her? and, did he intend for her to die?" He said, "The basis of the trial is this, it is for the prosecution to prove its case. One can not look into the mind of a man, so we have to prove it from the evidence. Intent has to be proved. If the defence can prove and put into the jury's mind reasonable doubt, the prisoner is entitled to acquittal."

Judge Walsh explained, "Reasonable doubt is when, after considering the Crown's case, the jury is not convinced. The jury does not have to look for fantastic doubt, the jury does not have to accept a fantastic story which nobody would believe. Look at the facts and sift them like reasonable men." He ruled out insanity and provocation as defences because the defence did not raise them. He concluded that if the jury could not find evidence of intent they could reduce the charge to manslaughter.

The jury took four hours to arrive at a decision. They reduced the charge to manslaughter and found Sweeney guilty. Sentencing was immediate. Sweeney stood and showed no emotion as he was sentenced to twenty years in prison.

November 4, 1950

Murder at St. Philip's

At 5:30 a.m. on Saturday, November 4, 1950, Tom Squires was stopped in front of Ethel Tucker's house in St. Philip's by several men looking for a taxi to St. John's. One of the men held out his hands and said, "My hands are full of blood. I was in a fight. Look, see, my face is all cut up." When Squires attempted to get down from the horse-drawn wagon to check on Ethel Tucker, a stout man warned, "If you're going to town, you better go on."

At 9 a.m. another neighbour, Eli Clarke, picked up three men and a woman at Ethel Tucker's and drove them to the Springdale Street area of St. John's. He became curious because each of the men were carrying parcels and one man was covered with blood. Upon his return to St. Philip's he dropped in to see how Ethel was and found her dead at the kitchen table. The place was covered in blood and the rooms in disarray. In the living room a pile of sheet music was strewn everywhere and only one sheet was left standing on the piano. It was "Too Many Parties, Too Many Pals."

Within an hour the police and pathologist were on the scene and an extensive investigation began. By next morning the police had arrested three men: Victor Rumsey, Max Evans and Herbert Hiscock. At first they were charged with robbery, but on December 22 this charge was upgraded to murder. Rumsey's mother Christine was so upset that she vowed to keep her Christmas tree up until Victor came home.

The trial got underway on January 29, 1951, just one day before Rumsey's eighteenth birthday. The trio were tried together with Jim Higgins defending Rumsey, Nath Noel defending Hiscock and Gordon Warren defending Evans. Acting for the Crown were H.P. Carter and Jim Power. The trial judge was Sir Albert Walsh.

The trial stirred sensational public interest. The court room was filled to capacity when the Crown's key witness, Irene McDonald testified. Irene, one of the four people at Ethel Tucker's house at the time of the murder, told the court that the men were not drunk and knew what they were doing. She said that she and Rumsey were frightened by the behaviour of Evans and Hiscock and they wanted to return to St. John's.

Near daybreak on November 4, Ethel had called Irene to a top story room and told her she was being robbed. Evans and Hiscock were rummaging through her belongings and putting them in bags. She said she was going to call the police. However, Hiscock moved behind her in the hallway and kicked her over the stairs. When Irene asked Evans and Hiscock to pick Ethel up, one of them replied, "Let the old sonofabitch stay there." When she asked the second time they carried her to the kitchen and stood her beside a furnace in a small room off the kitchen. Meanwhile, the lights went out and Evans and Hiscock began tossing things around the room. Irene and Rumsey ran outside and Hiscock and Evans followed. This was when Tom Squires stopped by and was told to keep moving. When they tried to get back inside, they discovered that Ethel had locked the door.

Hiscock shouted, "The old sonofabitch is not dead yet." He forced the door open. Hiscock demanded that Ethel pass over her money, and when she refused he punched her in the face and she fell to the floor. While she lay motionless on the floor Evans tossed burning paper onto her clothing. Rumsey tried with both hands to put the fire out and Evans joined in.

After threatening to burn Ethel to death Evans told the others he was going to have intercourse with her. Irene McDonald said she warned him to leave the woman alone, then went into another room. She returned when Rumsey called out, "Come out, Irene, and see what Max is doing." She found Evans lying beside Tucker with his pants open and her clothing pushed up over her waist. Irene said, "I told Evans if he did not get up I would kill him. I picked up the flat iron and I was going to hit him. He then got up and went to the front room. A few minutes later Hiscock grabbed Miss Tucker by the shoulders and lifted her to a chair near the kitchen table." Irene told the court that Hiscock threatened Ethel Tucker while they were locked outside. She quoted Hiscock as shouting, "I'll finish her when I get in."

The prosecutor attempted to discredit McDonald's testimony. He asked Irene if she had an argument with Hiscock before the visit to Ethel Tucker's and she said, "Yes." She testified that she accused Hiscock of being the father of her child and they argued over it. The prosecutor then asked why she had not helped Miss Tucker up after she was thrown over the stairs and she answered, "I was frightened."

Vic Rumsey's testimony was similar to Irene McDonald's. He was arrested on the morning of November 4 and taken to RCMP Offices on Kenna's Hill. He testified that the police corporal threatened him and tried hard to intimidate him. He said every time he tried to tell what happened the corporal would call him a liar. Rumsey said that when he told

Police he couldn't remember certain parts of what happened that night, the corporal threatened, "I'll give you something to refresh your memory."

Rumsey also recalled that he heard Hiscock going down the stairs and shouting, "Get out of my way." He remembered seeing Miss Tucker's head strike the coal bucket in the kitchen as she fell. He said when they picked her up and sat her by the table he thought she was still alive.

Hiscock testified that he tried to prevent violence. When someone said that Evans had a knife, he went to Evans and took an ice pick from him. He said he then searched him for a knife but didn't find one. He said he also helped put out the flames on Miss Tucker's clothing. He remembered nothing after that.

Evans was upset with the testimony his friends had given in court and when he took the stand he said to them, "You are all trying to hang me." He added, "I did not see anyone kick Miss Tucker down the stairs," though he did hear the sound of someone coming down the stairs. He said he found Miss Tucker at the foot of the stairs and he and Hiscock helped her to the kitchen. He strongly denied assaulting Ethel Tucker. Before leaving the stand he raised a question, "Why did Hiscock stop the man from coming into the house? Let the truth come out. If I did it I would gladly tell. I would not let the two young fellows to be charged with anything."

Dr. Joseph Josephson testified that the victim had died from shock brought on by the injuries suffered. He explained that most of the injuries could have been caused by the fall over the stairs but there were some caused by being hit and kicked. Dr. Josephson gave evidence regarding the question of a sexual assault having taken place. He said medical testing confirmed that Ethel Tucker had not been sexually assaulted the night of the murder.

The three defence lawyers then summed up their cases. Nath Noel suggested Irene McDonald was an accomplice and should not be believed. She participated in the robbery and told the three men where to find a screwdriver to force open a trunk. He concluded that the only evidence that Hiscock kicked Tucker down the stairs was that given by McDonald.

Jim Higgins told the jury that Rumsey was innocent of any part in the death of Ethel Tucker. He said Rumsey tried to protect her on several occasions and only got crumbs from the robbery. He said it was not the kind of loot that one would kill for. Higgins explained that Rumsey had not planned on visiting Tucker that night and had just made a bad decision by joining the others.

Gordon Warren defended Evans, pointing out that medical evidence contradicted Macdonald's and Rumsey's claim that Tucker had been sexually assaulted. He said the Doctors were quite clear in stating that sexual assault had not taken place. He said the victim was drunk and could have fallen over the stairs. Warren also suggested that Irene McDonald was an accomplice and could not be believed.

With the summaries concluded, the Judge addressed the jury. He explained, "If there is any reasonable doubt in your mind as to the guilt, any doubt that the accused killed the deceased, or did it without the state of mind required by law, the prosecution has not proven its case and the accused is entitled to an acquittal of murder, and in this case, you may reduce the charge to manslaughter in the case of each of the accused.

"In the criminal code, homicide is given as the killing of a person by another directly or indirectly by any means whatsoever. Then homicide is defined in two ways: homicide which is culpable and homicide which is not culpable. Homicide is culpable when it consists of the killing of any person by an unlawful act, either murder or manslaughter."

The Chief Justice then explained the circumstances under which all three defendants could be found guilty of murder. He said, "If in a robbery you strike a person, even if you do not mean to actually kill him, and death does not occur, you are held responsible for your action. It is for you to say whether the blow by the stove was given to try and extract from her where her money was. If you find the intent to rob, you must decide whether the violence was caused for the intent of robbery or in connection with flight. If several persons form together to commit a robbery, each is equally guilty, If drunkenness is found, murder can be reduced to manslaughter. If you find that Hiscock killed Mary Ethel Tucker, went to do it, for committing a robbery, you have to return a verdict of guilty as charged. If the other accused assisted each other they are equally guilty. You have three verdicts to consider: guilty of murder, guilty of manslaughter or not guilty."

The jury took an hour to bring back a verdict of guilty of manslaughter. Because the same verdict was required against all three due to circumstances of the case, the jury did not want to see young Rumsey hanged. This influenced the decision to reduce the verdict from murder to manslaughter with a recommendation of mercy for Victor Rumsey. Evans and Hiscock got a twenty year sentence, while Rumsey received ten years.

When Rumsey was released from prison he visited jury chairman Joe Ashley to thank him for showing mercy in the jury's verdict. Ashley offered to help him, gave him some money, and then found him a job.

April 14, 1954

Valdmanis

The most sensational white collar criminal case in New-foundland history began on April 14, 1954 when RCMP in New Brunswick arrested a man who just a short time before had been the second most powerful man in Newfoundland, next to Premier Joe Smallwood.

Dr. Alfred Valdmanis, the former Director of Economic Development in Newfoundland, was brought to St. John's and charged with defrauding the provincial government of nearly a half-million dollars. The warrant which led to his arrest was sparked by a complaint made by Premier Small-wood. The relationship between the two had soured when Joey learned that Valdmanis was abusing his position. Vald-manis had began spending more and more time in Montreal away from his job; he incurred large travelling expenses and, without consulting the premier, had opened and staffed a Montreal office for the Newfoundland and Labrador Devel-opment Corporation. Along with padding his expense ac-count, Valdmanis collected three months' double salary. He used NALCO funds to purchase a new car and four tires, and rented a suite at the Mount Royal Hotel. He used NALCO funds to purchase custom built and antique furniture.

Smallwood demanded and received his resignation. Sev-eral months later Smallwood obtained information that the doctor had been defrauding the government of large amounts of money. He made a complaint to the RCMP upon which they acted swiftly. While I was researching this story for my book *Too Many Parties, Too Many Pals*, Smallwood told me, "Up to the time I asked Valdmanis for his resignation I had no reason to suspect him of personal dishonesty. Shortly after his resignation my suspicions were aroused and I undertook some quiet investigating. The investigation confirmed my suspicions and I passed my information over to the RCMP."

Joey described his move as, "Perhaps one of the hardest decisions I shall probably ever be called upon to make. The affair was a great personal blow. I had to swallow everything I ever said publicly in his favour. The man was brilliant, superlatively brilliant. He had everything."

Valdmanis had an intriguing background. At the age of twenty-nine he had already held four portfolios in the Latvian Government; several university degrees; spoke several languages; had acted as President of Latvia in the absence of the president and had been decorated by the King of Sweden.

When the Russians invaded his country he organized a resistance group, for which he was sent to a firing squad. However, the Germans invaded Latvia and rescued him before the order could be carried out. The Germans restored him to his political position and when he refused to cooperate with them he was again arrested and sent to a firing squad. While awaiting his fate he was tortured with piano wire by the Nazis. Through the intervention of the King of Sweden, Valdmanis was once again rescued but this time he was sent to Berlin. Because of his expertise in finance he was assigned a position on the staff of Dr. Helmut Schacht, Hitler's Economic Adviser.

During the bombing of Berlin, he led the rescue of 800 people from a bombed building. In the process he suffered permanent damage to his eyes. After the war he served on the staffs of Field Marshall Montgomery and later General Walter Smith of the U.S.Army as special adviser. Two years later he went to Switzerland to serve with the International Refugee Organization.

In 1949, Smallwood attempted to stem the tide of emigration from Newfoundland by launching an economic development program. He sought an expert in this field to head the effort. Commenting on why he didn't seek a Newfoundland businessman for the job, Joey said, "It was useless to turn to the businessmen of Newfoundland. Most of them were scrambling around like henhawks eyeing a chicken coop, for their share of the millions of dollars in family allowances and other cash pouring in from Ottawa."

After several attempts to attract the right person Smallwood was introduced to Dr. Alfred Valdmanis by Canada's Trade Minister, C.D.Howe. Valdmanis came highly recommended. Among his supporters were the Lady Davis Foundation, C.D.Howe and Dr. Hugh Keenleyside, head of a United Nations Commission. Smallwood hired Valdmanis at a salary of ten thousand dollars a year. Within three years he had brought sixteen new industries to Newfoundland and his salary had increased to thirty thousand dollars yearly.

Throughout this period, Valdmanis was milking the German investors. He used the German firms of MIAG and Benno Shilde to defraud the Newfoundland Government of $470,000. Contrary to information contained in John Crosbie's recent book and in the CBC Program "East of Canada," the RCMP investigation determined that Valdmanis negotiated these deals in his basement office at Colonial Building, and was careful to make sure no witnesses were present. On one occasion when two friends of Valdmanis were present in the office, the doctor invited the industrialists to another office to negotiate the kick-back. Premier Smallwood was never present at any of these transactions and had absolutely no knowledge of Valdmanis' illegal activity until the story began unravelling in 1954.

While Valdmanis was on bail from these charges an interesting situation took place which has been a source of many erroneous accounts of the Valdmanis crimes. In June,1954 the *Evening Telegram* printed the following: "Dr. Alfred Valdmanis, having shaken the hand of Counsel, Gordon F. Higgins, was re-arrested this morning from Higgins' home and taken not to jail, but to the Newfoundland Hotel, literally as a guest of Hon. Attorney General Leslie R. Curtis."

This prompted Chief Justice Sir Brian Dunfield on behalf of other Supreme Court Justices to warn the press. He said, "I think it is about time that the publicity agencies we have in our midst took advice from their lawyers to the limitations binding on them as to their comments on proceedings in this court."

No doubt this episode was the root of stories over later years that Valdmanis received special treatment and was allowed to serve some of his time at Hotel Newfoundland. In actual fact, there was a legitimate reason for the doctor to be imprisoned in a hotel. This second arrest was based on civil action and not criminal charges. Under civil law, the person who applies for a warrant for the arrest of a man is responsible for the man and his upkeep. Consequently, since the Government ordered the arrest in an effort to recover the stolen monies, the Government had to pay for the hotel bill and police guards. When the hotel became too expensive, Valdmanis was moved to the Cochrane Hotel.

The investigation into this fraud case involved the RCMP, FBI and Interpol. Evidence showed Valdmanis acted independently. However, the detailed account of how he operated and the long chain of actions to hide his deeds were not made public, because Valdmanis pleaded guilty to one charge and the second charge was dropped. I believe it was not until I obtained access to the court evidence and police investigations in 1981 that the full and accurate background to the scandal was made public. I published the full story in my book *Too Many Parties, Too Many Pals*, which at the time of writing this book, is still on the market.

Dr. Valdmanis turned over all his assets, valued at $568,750.80 to the Newfoundland Government, and had the government's civil suit dropped. The sale of these assets realized a little over thirteen thousand dollars. When Valdmanis was asked what he did with the money he answered, "Blackmail." There were suggestions that he was being blackmailed by two fellow Latvians over claims that Valdmanis had a sinister involvement with the Nazis during World War II.

After his release from prison, Valdmanis left Newfoundland and never returned. He died in a car accident in Alberta in 1970.

January 10, 1956
The Escape of Jim Robbins

Just before five p.m. on January 10, 1956, inmates Jim Robbins and Gerald Hanlon propped a door against the prison wall and made a successful escape from Her Majesty's Prison in St. John's. Hanlon's freedom was short-lived; the police caught him on Murphy's Avenue. Robbins had better luck. He evaded police a lot longer and managed to arouse the kind of sentiment that had made Philip Brady a local folk-hero a half century before.

The thirty-six year old Robbins, who had been deported from the United States in 1948 after serving seven of ten years for manslaughter, had a record of violence. City police were quick to advise the public that he was considered dangerous. At the time of his escape he was serving a thirty month sentence for robbery and assault. His victim was Cyril Murphy, a Canadian Customs official.

The robbery and assault charge had been tried in March, 1955. Throughout the hearing the prisoner displayed the arrogance and contempt for the Justice system that was apparent throughout his criminal life. After being found guilty he shouted at Magistrate Hugh O'Neill, "Go to your chamber and look into your conscience and ask from the bottom of your heart whether I am innocent."

O'Neill replied, "You are not safe to be at large."

The prisoner answered, "I still maintain my innocence."

When O'Neill sentenced Robbins to thirty months in jail, Robbins shouted,"Did Carter [the prosecutor] influence your decision?" O'Neill said, "No, he only brought out the facts."

Jim Robbins was just as unruly in prison. He was a constant source of problems for prison guards. On one occasion when he was causing an uproar in his cell, the warden, Otto Kelland, fired two shots into the cell floor. Undeterred, Robbins faced Kelland and, pointing his index finger towards the centre of his head, shouted, "If you want to stop me the next time, you better shoot there."

After escaping HMP, Robbins evaded police for more than a year and attracted nation wide publicity. He moved to Toronto and rented an apartment next to a hideout used a year earlier by Leonard Jackson, who was later hanged for the murder of Detective Sergeant Edmond Tong of the Toronto Police Force.

Just a couple of weeks before his capture, Robbins made

the list of the ten most-wanted men in Canada. The *Weekend Magazine* featured pictures of the ten in a special feature article. Meanwhile, in St. John's, the London Theatre resurrected the folk hero image of Brady and tried to turn Robbins into a similar type of hero. The group put off a play featuring many of the ideas used to depict Brady's escapades.

In Toronto, Robbins worked with a pipe distributing firm, using the alias James Parker. A rowdy Christmas party in 1956 led to his recapture. Neighbours complained to police and when they attempted to break up the party Robbins was arrested. However, the police had no idea who he was until a fingerprint match identified him.

Elizabeth Tapp, his landlady, expressed surprise when told of her boarder's true identity. She said, "He was a steady worker and was well liked at the factory." Toronto police dropped disorderly conduct charges against Robbins and shipped him back to St. John's. After completing his prison term, he moved to Montreal. In 1963 he was again arrested and charged with the non-capital murder of Constance Mary McGee, whom he beat to death.

During this trial, Robbins had the court in an almost continuous uproar. On several occasions he was ordered out of court because of his arrogant conduct. The Court appointed Edwin Murphy, Q.C. and John Hannon as defence lawyers for Robbins. The Crown was represented by Kenneth MacKay.

Throughout the trial Robbins refused to co-operate with his lawyers and even took the witness stand against their advice, maintaining the trial should be declared a mistrial. Before being removed from the witness stand, he hurled insults at his own lawyers and at the presiding judge, Francois Caron. When he later returned to court he was a model of good behaviour. He told the court, "I'm not asking for pity, only for justice." He claimed there had been numerous ir-regularities in his trial and the judge should have declared it a mistrial. Some of the irregularities he referred to included "witnesses being coached by the police, and the failure of my lawyers to bring to court certain witnesses I wanted to have heard."

During his testimony, Judge Caron showed great pa-tience with the accused. He allowed him to go on uninter-rupted as he referred to 'kangaroo justice' in the Coroner's Court, and made references to such widely separated inci-dents as the assassination of President Kennedy and the Coffey murder case. He also said his lawyers had suggested he plead guilty to manslaughter, telling him he would serve about six years of what would probably be a ten year sen-tence.

At this point, Robbins' voice became louder as he faced the jury saying, "I refused to do this. There is no question of manslaughter in this case. You either find me guilty of non-capital murder or acquit me. And don't forget I am entitled to the full benefit of the doubt."

In anticipation of the Crown bringing his record into court, Robbins outlined his record for the jury. He also ex-plained that on the day of McGee's death, he had been drinking with some friends. The drinking was interrupted by a visit to a sick friend in hospital. Leaving the hospital, he went to a McGill Street club and continued to drink. He said, "I met Connie in the club. There was a fight there and that's all I remembered until I woke up."

He said the woman was beside him in bed and was breathing heavily. He asked neighbours to call a doctor and ambulance. The woman died later that day in hospital.

Robbins was found guilty as charged and sentenced to life imprisonment. Even in the court cells, he had acted unruly. During the lunch break before sentencing, he got into an argument with another prisoner and raked him across the eyes with a metal object. The prisoner was taken to hospital for treatment.

Commenting on the jury's decision Judge Caron said, "The jury's verdict is fully justified by the evidence." Before he could finish his thought Robbins loudly interjected, "This is a travesty of justice. I hope everyone sleeps well tonight."

But Judge Caron got in the last word. He said, "You were listened to as long as you wanted to talk. I have no alternative under the law but to impose a life sentence on you."

June 25, 1957
The Sand Pits Murders

A bizarre episode in Newfoundland criminal history took place during the summer of 1957. Its surprise ending created a mystery that has remained unsolved for almost forty years. Many around St. John's remember it as the perfect crime.

The mystery first came to light when three boys playing in the Sand Pits off Elizabeth Avenue discovered a bundle with the charred remains of a baby. The police were called to the scene and began gathering evidence. Sgt. Ron Evans recalled, "The baby was burned considerably and covered with charred papers, tissues and bits of clothing." The investigation was turned over to the RCMP because Elizabeth Avenue was outside the city at the time.

During the autopsy at the City Morgue, police made another gruesome discovery. A second bundle taken from the scene was opened by Corporal Pat Noonan and the charred remains of a second baby was found. Noonan described the condition, "It was in a decomposed state and dead for some time. It was in a mummified condition, flattened to a thickness of about three inches and dried and hard like a piece of board."

Who were the children? Were they alive before being burned? Who did it? Were there any witnesses? Why? These were some questions confronting the RCMP as they took charge of the investigation that night.

Their investigation took off the next morning after news reports of the mystery hit the airways. Al Downey, city taxi driver, recalled taking a woman from 92 Queen's Road to the Sand Pits several nights before. She brought with her a carton of what she described as old clothes. He told police she asked him to wait as she set fire to the box and left only after the fire had burned out.

Based on the driver's information Police arrested thirty-seven-year-old Louise Dunn of 92 Queen's Rd. They searched her apartment and gathered evidence including papers from the fireplace and some old clothing. Although two bodies were recovered, she was only charged with dumping the body of one child and attempting to burn it.

City lawyer Sam Hawkins was hired to defend Dunn. After hearing her story he expressed doubts about the legality of the charge. He explained that the charge was related to a mother disposing of her child's body. Louise had been examined by a Doctor and it was determined she had not recently given birth. Louise told Hawkins she had not been pregnant since 1953.

Louise denied having any knowledge of the affair. She explained that the blood evidence police took from her bed was from a pregnancy in 1953. Hawkins questioned the police line-up and asked what description the police had prior to arresting his client. Sgt. Hugh Coady answered that he was told the address of the woman and that she was from the mainland. Louise Dunn was the only mainlander in that house.

When police mentioned that they took a large sum of money from the accused at the time of the arrest the defence objected, claiming, "it is irrelevant and could prejudice some of the issues for the defence." Magistrate Hugh O'Neill agreed.

The pathologist, Dr. Joseph Josephson, caused a stir in the court room when he suggested the babies had been murdered before being dumped at the Sand Pits. Both had been born full-term and were alive at birth. He could find no blood traces on which to base any conclusion of relationship. Dr. Josephson noted that death by natural causes was possible but it was likely that the children had been smothered.

The crown relied on the evidence of Al Downey for its case. They argued that he had credibility because he was able to take them to the exact site and he identified Louise Dunn in the police line-up. When asked if the accused had explained what she was doing, the cab driver answered, she said she was burning some soiled clothes which she didn't want to throw in the garbage. The next day the *Daily News* head line read, "Fingered by Body Burning Trial Starts."

There was public speculation that the babies had been killed to cover up the involvement with prostitutes of some prominent names. However, no evidence surfaced at trial to support that belief.

Near the end of the trial Hawkins called a surprise witness and drew the ire of the prosecution for not giving proper notice. The witness, John Maloney, a contractor with offices at Argentia and St. John's, provided the accused with an alibi for the night it was claimed she disposed of the bodies. He testified Louise Dunn was with him from 10:30 p.m. to one a.m. on June 25. The defence concluded she was innocent because here was proof she had not been at the Sand Pits that night.

Although Dunn testified in Court that she was with Maloney at the Pioneer Restaurant on the night of the crime, she had previously given two separate statements to police that she went home at eleven forty-five p.m. that night and had not seen anyone she knew.

When the prosecution questioned the discrepancies between her evidence in court and the police statements, she answered that she had not read the statements, and she felt no obligation to tell them anything about Maloney.

Louise Dunn told the court she had known Maloney for three years, but when cross examined testified she did not know his address or telephone number. She said she had been meeting with him about every ten days and that he would make the contact.

When asked if she knew the cab driver who identified her she stated, she did, adding that he had tried to set her up with servicemen on occasions before, but she ignored him. She said she had never been in his taxi. Dunn stuck to her story that she was at the Pioneer Restaurant with Maloney on June 25. She denied any knowledge of the dead children. When pressed by the Crown to disclose her source of income she said she received support from her ex-husband and operated a small business modelling and selling clothes.

In his summary at the end of the trial, Hawkins argued that the Crown made no attempt to prove the child belonged to Louise Dunn. He claimed the entire case revolved around the identity issue and that the taxi driver was not a credible witness. Hawkins contended that the evidence of Maloney was sufficient to acquit his client. He added that medical evidence showed that Louise had not given birth during the four week period prior to the discovery of the charred bodies.

He concluded saying, "It is dangerous to convict when there is an indication that the witness is an accomplice."

The Crown's summary argued that there was sufficient evidence to convict. The prosecutor told the judge that Al Downey, the driver, was credible and he was present when the bodies were burned. He said the defence alibi should not be believed because the accused made no effort to present this evidence to the police. He said, "The defence of alibi ought to be introduced at the earliest point as a rule of expediency. She made no attempt to tell anyone of her alibi."

After reviewing the evidence Magistrate Hugh O'Neill said he was left with no choice but to acquit. Louise Dunn thanked her lawyer, tossed her hair back and smiled at police officers as she left the court room. The trial was over but the crime was not solved. Two murders had been committed and despite efforts by the *Evening Telegram* through its editorial pages, the case was not reopened and no person has yet been charged with the murder of the two infants.

November 7, 1958

Constable Hooey Shot

During the early morning hours of November 7, 1958, radio news bulletins were being flashed across the province describing a spectacular but tragic shootout at the Harbour View Cafe in Botwood.

The confrontation between RCMP officers and the Chinese occupants of the cafe had broken out at about eleven p.m. and was still in progress. One police officer was already dead, two Botwood men had been wounded, the building was ablaze, and RCMP reinforcements were arriving from Grand Falls and Corner Brook. Some local residents, caught up in the excitement of the battle, armed themselves with rifles and went to the assistance of the RCMP. Mr. and Mrs. A. Arklie, who occupied the house next to the cafe, served hot coffee and toast to police throughout the twelve-hour shoot-out.

This episode in Newfoundland criminal history began on the evening of November 6th, when Ursula Canning, a waitress at the cafe, reported to the RCMP that she had been appearing for work throughout the week but each time she did, the place was closed. Miss Canning suspected something was seriously wrong.

RCMP Sergeant Red Bowen and Constables Terry Hooey and Bob Healey set off on the routine investigation to find out if anything was wrong at the Harbour View Cafe. After failing to get a reply to their heavy knocking at the front entrance, the police officers forced their way into the cafe. It was almost nine p.m. and the place was in darkness. The trio checked out the restaurant section of the building and, finding no one there, made their way up the stairway to the living quarters of the building.

Slowly they opened the door to a bedroom where they believed the owner, fifty-seven-year-old Jim Ling, to be. Ling didn't wait for conversation. As the door opened he fired a blast from his shotgun which caught Hooey in the chest. The other two officers carried Hooey downstairs and in a matter of minutes Constable Terry Hooey of Havelock, Ontario was dead.

Sergeant Bowen immediately called for reinforcements and the siege of the Harbour View began. Ling had barricaded himself in the upstairs bedroom, and made it plain he was not coming out without a fight. Gunfire erupted from the upstairs window, which sent the police and spectators scurrying for shelter.

At this stage, police were not certain how many people were in the room. There was speculation that Ling's twenty-one-year-old son Kenneth was with his father. The Chinese man had a 22 calibre rifle, a 12 gauge shotgun and a .303 Enfield rifle.

The cracking sound of gunfire attracted hundreds of spectators as word of the shootout rapidly spread throughout the town. Some of the hundreds of spectators had armed themselves and exchanged shots with Ling in an effort to help police.

In view of the seriousness of the situation, the RCMP sent reinforcements from Grand Falls and Corner Brook. Spotlights were also set up around the cafe. RCMP Inspector Argent brought tear gas bombs from Corner Brook.

When the shooting subsided, police attempted to persuade Ling to give himself up. When this failed, police tossed a tear gas bomb through the window. Ling reacted with gunfire. About three or four such bombs were tossed into the window. Ling was determined to resist the police. He managed to toss one of the bombs back through the window at the police below. It is believed that one of the bombs exploded and caused the fire which eventually gutted the upstairs portion of the cafe.

The Botwood Fire Department had been called in by the police at the beginning of the standoff. When Fire Chief Graham LeDrew made a move to lead his Brigade in their effort to stop the fire, Ling shot him. The blast smashed the bone in LeDrew's arm. Particles of flesh and bone were embedded in the corner of the building when the slug went through his arm and then into the building. Another fireman, Gordon Locke junior, was also hit by a shotgun blast. He was not seriously injured.

There were strong southwest winds blowing in over the harbour that night and the firemen had a battle on their hands to prevent the fire from spreading. Following the fire, some well-intentioned citizens caused the police some concern. Several male residents of Botwood got into a downstairs section of the building. All were armed. One man had to be held back by police when he made a dash to go upstairs and shoot it out with the Chinese man. The police took control of the situation and instantly removed the armed men from the building. The firemen kept the blaze under control and confined to the upstairs area.

Some time passed without any indication of activity from the barricaded Ling room. The RCMP and firemen moved into the building and up to the second story room, where they found the dead bodies of Ling and his son. Kenneth's body was found against the inside wall of the bedroom, and his father was lying across a chesterfield in the room. Speculation throughout the town was that Ling had shot and killed his son earlier that week and then barricaded himself along with the dead body inside the upstairs bedroom.

Constable Hooey was the first police officer to be killed in the line of duty in Newfoundland.

March 10, 1959

Constable William Moss

The 1959 strike by the International Woodworkers of America is remembered well in Newfoundland history because of the violence by strikers which culminated in the death of Royal Newfoundland Constabulary Officer William Moss. The strike was called on December 31, 1958. Over the following weeks the union waged a bitter campaign of violence and total disregard for the law. Workers had reason to be angry, because the employers refused to accept an arbitration board's decision in favour of the employees.

During the initial stages of the strike, there was strong public support for workers and the Provincial Government remained outside the dispute. However, IWA support eroded as strikers began ignoring the law and turning to violence. By February 7 the violence escalated to an armed attack on helpless men sleeping in their woods camps. At two-thirty a.m. IWA picketers beat the men with sticks and forced them, in many cases without clothing, into below freezing temperatures outside. One man was knocked unconscious. The following day 104 IWA members were arrested and pressure began mounting to have the Provincial Government intervene.

Support for intervention came from labour groups, church leaders, members of the press and the general public. Newfoundland's Attorney General urged strikers not to break the law or to commit acts of violence. He pleaded for them to keep the peace. The warnings were ignored and the violence continued.

On February 12, the Provincial Government amended its

labour laws. The IWA was decertified and a new union was set up to replace them. Provisions were also included to outlaw unions controlled by gangsters from setting up in Newfoundland. (The Newfoundland Government was strongly influenced by the Senate Rackets Committee in the U.S. which identified criminals involved in top union positions there.) The legislation received unanimous approval in the legislature.

Despite Government efforts to stop them and dwindling public support, the IWA fought hard to keep the strike going. When some of their own members turned away in the Badger area, the IWA brought in outsiders. The Newfoundland Constabulary sent reinforcements for the RCMP and additional RCMP support was requested through the Federal Government. At first the Federal Justice Minister approved reinforcements but this was cancelled when Prime Minister Diefenbaker intervened. This action brought a new dimension to the dispute.

On March 3, Premier J.R. Smallwood, referring to a legal contract signed several years before between the two Governments, launched a law-suit against the Federal Government for breach of contract. While the controversy continued, more Constabulary members were sent to central Newfoundland, leaving the City of St. John's with minimum police protection.

On March 10, while Max Lane was at Grand Falls setting up the new union to replace the IWA, Constable William Moss was among the police officers patrolling the streets at Badger. The police formed groups and marched together through the streets. During the effort a scuffle broke out between strikers and police. When the police broke formation there was much confusion. Strikers ran in all directions and at least three officers were hit with sticks. A birch junk was used to hit Moss in the head and he fell to the ground. The injured man was rushed to the Grand Falls Hospital but passed away thirty-two hours later.

Ronald Laing of Bonne Bay was charged with the murder. He was held in custody while awaiting trial. Three months later he was acquitted by a jury of killing Constable Moss. Nobody has ever been convicted for causing the death of the young police officer.

The Royal Newfoundland Constabulary has honoured the memory of Constable William Moss by having a special plaque dedicated to his memory at the front of police headquarters off Parade Street. In addition the RNC sponsors the Moss Memorial Softball tournament each year to remember Constable William Moss, and the dedication to duty and the sacrifice that police officers are sometimes called upon to make in the performance of their duties.

March 20, 1960

The Murder of Joan Ash

On March 20, 1960, nineteen year old Joan Ash of Carbonear boarded the bus near her home. She had been accompanied on her visit home with co-worker and friend Vivian Chard. Joan, who was employed at the old General Hospital on Forest Road, was returning to her boarding house in St. John's, but she never made it. Minutes after leaving the bus in St. John's she was bludgeoned to death.

During the visit, Joan told her parents of threats made against her life but said she was not concerned about them. The threats had been made by twenty-eight-year-old Donald

Stone, whom Joan had dated on several occasions but had broken off with after being told he was "oversexed." What Joan didn't know was that Donald Stone had psychiatric problems and was an ex-patient of the Hospital for Mental and Nervous Diseases. Stone was from Bryant's Cove but was boarding on Carter's Hill in St. John's.

When the bus stopped at Harbour Grace to pick up passengers, Donald Stone boarded and sat opposite Joan and Vivian. He exposed himself all the way to St. John's. The girls ignored him, but Joan talked loudly about a new boy friend. Vivian later told police she thought Joan wanted Stone to hear.

The bus dropped the girls off behind the Hotel New-foundland. Joan and Vivian walked together, close behind was Anne Hall who also worked at the Hospital, and behind her was Donald Stone. Hall noticed Stone as he quickened his pace, passed her and grabbed Joan Ash by the throat. She recalled he threw Joan to the ground and dragged her towards a nearby building. Vivian heard Joan cry out "Vivian!" Vivian and Anne ran to the hospital to call police. Vivian recalled that she considered trying to help but was scared because Joan had told her earlier that Stone had a gun.

The attack on the young girl was vicious. By the time her assailant had completely vented his anger, only the bone at the base of her skull remained unbroken. Her face bore almost the full brunt of the attack. It was swollen and distorted and a partial plate with several teeth was driven down her throat. She had struggled but was easily overpowered by Stone. When Stone was satisfied his victim was dead he remained near the body and told several people passing by that he killed her and requested them to call the police.

Sgts. Vince Nugent and Don Randell responded to the calls and had no trouble getting a confession from Stone.

Donald Stone described the attack to them. "I went up behind her and grabbed her by the throat with my hands, I had gloves on," he said. He added, "I knocked her to the ground and tried to strangle her. I kept her down and kicked her around the head. When I stopped kicking I figured she was dead. I remember her saying, 'God damn you, Stone.'

Stone's statement to police, which was read in court during the trial, stated, "I feel sick all the time and have no control over my feelings. I have been in the Mental Hospital twice. The first time it was for three months and the second time for two months." Jim Higgins represented Stone at the trial. Higgins had a very successful trial record. He had represented eighteen defendants in first degree murder cases and had not lost a case. In this case Higgins argued his client was not guilty by reason of insanity. On June 1, 1960 the jury returned a verdict of not guilty by reason of insanity. Stone was committed to the Mental Hospital. At one point after his arrest Stone said he would rather die than be sent there. Just months after being admitted, Stone suffered a massive heart attack and died.

June 1960

The C.O.D. Murder

The body of Marjorie Scott lies peacefully in the Anglican Cemetery at St. John's. The grave doesn't attract any special attention and the name Marjorie Scott has no special meaning to the hundreds who pass it by each year for the annual flower service. Yet Marjorie Scott was the victim of a crime that set in motion one of the most expensive police investigations in Ontario history, a two-province-wide police investigation and a Canada-wide warrant for the arrest of a man suspected of murder. The Scott mystery attracted media attention in the United States as well as Canada and became known as "The C.O.D. Murder."

The bizarre mystery surrounding the Scott case began in June 1960, when Tom Donovan, a Canadian National Express agent at Argentia, detected a foul odour coming from a trunk being held at the station. The trunk had arrived $17.68 C.O.D. at Argentia, addressed to a Mrs. Williams. However, when nobody claimed it, CN placed it in storage. If not claimed in six months it would have been opened and auctioned off.

The mystery trunk had been shipped from Toronto on May 4th and had arrived at Argentia on May 16th marked 'Fragile Handle With Care.' As days passed with the trunk remaining unclaimed an offensive odour began spreading through the building. It became so bad that Donovan was forced to open the trunk. He was horrified to discover the body of a dead woman wrapped in a blanket.

Donovan described the victim as blonde, five feet tall, weighing about 115 pounds, and wearing a white dress. He reported the finding to the RCMP, and a murder mystery that monopolized the news for nearly two months in Newfoundland and Ontario began. Police found bloodstains on the trunk but nothing to indicate the cause of death. The autopsy determined the victim was about thirty years old but could not explain the cause of death.

RCMP Inspector D.O. Bartrum of the St. John's Detachment arranged for the organs from the body to be sent to the RCMP lab in Sackville, New Brunswick for detailed examination.

While medical experts laboured to determine the cause of

death, an intensive effort was being carried out throughout Newfoundland and Ontario to identify the victim. At first it was believed that the victim was a young woman from Harbour Grace. Her mother advised police that she believed the dead girl was her daughter, who had married an American serviceman ten years earlier. Police investigated this lead and found that her daughter was alive and well and living in the southern United States.

Speculation that the woman was a Newfoundlander heightened when a St. John's dentist described the woman's bridgework as 'local work.' Shortly after this, a man in Lethbridge, Bonavista Bay, reported to police that his daughter had been missing for eighteen months. However, the description did not fit that of the girl found in the trunk.

While Toronto police followed up every lead, doctors at Argentia determined after examining the victim's false teeth that a congenital defect had left a gap in the woman's own upper teeth. This information was given much media attention in hope that a dentist somewhere would recall such a patient.

Weeks passed and still the victim's identity and cause of death remained a mystery. A soldier stationed at Barrie,Ontario reported his wife missing, but once again, the description did not fit that of the victim. Meanwhile, police were making some headway. Police in Toronto tracked down a railway employee who remembered helping a man unload a trunk meeting the description of the one shipped to Argentia on May 4th. While this lead brought police closer to solving the mystery, other leads continued to develop, but most were dead ends. Police questioned an American serviceman who had married a Newfoundland girl who had been reported missing. The man was located on a U.S. military base and when asked if he would be making arrangements to return to

Newfoundland for the funeral replied, "I wouldn't go off the base to see her."

By mid-June the RCMP fingerprint division in Ottawa had identified the victim as thirty-seven year old Marjorie Scott. Her fingerprints were on file because she had been in trouble with the police in 1944. The victim had married Clement Scott while still in her teens. Both got into trouble with police and served time in prison. Marjorie served three months on a theft and morals charge while her husband served eighteen months for the same offence. Clement Scott committed suicide by hanging himself while serving his sentence at New Westminster, B.C. in 1958.

The investigation was now left to the Ontario Police because it was apparent that the crime had been committed there.One hundred police officers were now involved in the investigation, yet the cause of death was still unknown. The media speculated that either strangulation or poisoning had caused Scott's death.

Police efforts began to pay off. They learned that on May 4 Leonard Eade, who had lived with Scott for about ten years, left the apartment he shared with her. It was the same day the trunk had been shipped from Toronto. Leonard was five feet six inches tall with brown hair and brown eyes. He was a machine operator by trade and had worked for some time as a seaman.

Police had reason to suspect foul play. Marjorie's sister informed them that she had received a telegram from Marjorie suggesting her life was in danger. This followed an earlier telephone call from an unidentified man in Toronto telling her that Marjorie was hooked on dope.

Meanwhile, a Toronto landlady identified the trunk. She recognized it as the one Scott used when she was evicted from her apartment. During the eviction process Scott had threatened the landlady with a gun.

As police were preparing to have a warrant issued for Eade's arrest, a letter appeared in the *Toronto Star* in the pal-advertisement section, which was signed by Leonard J. Eade with the Scott address. Robbie Tremblay, a truck driver, reported to police that he had delivered a trunk fitting the description of the one used to transport Scott's body to Newfoundland. He said a man paid him five dollars to deliver the trunk to CN. A few days later the Toronto Metropolitan Police offered a $1,000 reward for information leading to the arrest and conviction of Leonard Eade.

Peter Campbell, a tenant in the apartment house where Scott had lived, reported he had overheard an argument between Scott and a man on May 3rd. He recalled the man shouted, "I'm going to kill you." The witness told police he saw Eade packing to leave the house the next day, and there was a gun sticking out from his clothing. Campbell added that a week later he took a call from Eade from Cleveland asking if anyone had been looking for him.

Acting on this information, Cleveland police apprehended Eade and passed him over to Ontario police. It seemed the mystery was solved. Eade told police that he choked Scott in their apartment following an argument the two had had in a Toronto bar earlier that night. Eade said he did not realize Scott was dead until the following morning, when he attempted to wake her. He consumed several bottles of wine as he sought a means of covering up his deed. It was during this drinking that he came up with the idea of putting the body in a trunk and sending it C.O.D. to Placentia, Newfoundland.

Just as it seemed the mystery was solved, an unexpected twist occurred. Dr. W.J. Deadmon of the attorney-general's department had examined and reported that there were no marks of external violence on the body. Crown Prosecutor Arthur O'Kein told the court that police had evidence that while the victim had died as a result of asphyxiation, there was no evidence she had been murdered. Charges of murder against Eade were dropped, ending one of the most intensive and expensive police manhunts in Ontario history.

December 17, 1964

RCMP Officer Shot

Near midnight on December 16, four prisoners—Melvin Young, Winston Noseworthy, James Thorne and John Snow—escaped from her majesty's Penitentiary in St. John's. They stole a car at Quidi Vidi, switched to another stolen vehicle on Topsail Road and headed west on the Trans Canada Highway. Near Whitbourne they broke through a police road block . The two RCMP officers at the road block gave chase and caught up with the escapees at Whitbourne.

The police tried to contain the escapees in the Whitbourne Avenue area while awaiting reinforcements. The prisoners jumped the police and during the scuffle a gun was wrestled from Constable Dave Keith. In response, Constable Robert Amey drew his gun. Keith recalled, "I believe Young told Amey to drop his gun. Then I heard a shot. I could see my gun move up a little in Young's hand. After the shot I looked at Constable Amey and I saw him put his hand up towards his chest. Then I saw him start to fall."

Amey put his hand on his chest and then fell to the snow-covered ground. Blood poured from his mouth and from the bullet wounds in his chest and back. Amey died almost instantly.

Keith said, "I went to Constable Amey and he was just about completely on the ground. I then took his revolver from him. There were constables running up the road towards us from where the police car had been parked. Before Amey was shot I hollered to them to watch it as Young had my gun." Young, meanwhile, ran into Barrett's store and took Fred Barrett hostage. He agreed to release his prisoner and give himself up only after Constable Keith agreed to empty his gun and drop it.

The four convicts were arrested and taken to the RCMP Whitbourne Detachment. Young discussed the shooting with the others in his cell. RCMP officers on guard that night stated that Young said, "I fired at his gun. I didn't know I hit him. Fucker! they can only hang you. That's first degree murder. He was just going to squeeze the trigger when I shot. I was going to fire at his legs first; then I fired at the gun."

The trial was held in Supreme Court at St. John's. The presiding judge was R.S. Furlong. The Crown was represented by Jim Power and William Gillies. Fintan Aylward represented the accused.

The Crown presented a strong case with several RCMP officers as witnesses and corroborating evidence. The defence argued that considering the downward trajectory of the bullet as outlined in the autopsy, Young would have had to be eleven feet tall to have shot Amey. Aylward suggested that because Police had drawn guns and there was an exchange of gunfire, one of the Police bullets might have accidently hit Amey. In response to this the prosecution suggested the bullet could have deflected. No expert witnesses on deflection were called by either side. When Young claimed that after he fired at Amey, the victim had walked to the side of Barrett's Store, the prosecution noted the autopsy stated that Amey died instantly.

In his summary, Aylward stated that Young was guilty of resisting arrest, escaping lawful custody and stealing a car along with other offenses. But he was not guilty of capital murder. He said there was excessive use of guns that day by the RCMP officers. Aylward claimed that if a more senior officer had been present that day, guns would not have been necessary in making the arrest. He told the jury that they must be morally certain that the bullet from Young's gun killed Amey. He pointed out that while the RCMP ballistics expert had identified the bullet presented in court as having come from Young's gun, there was no microscopic evidence of any human tissue on it. The prosecution concluded that the evidence by RCMP and civilian witnesses clearly showed that Young had shot and killed Constable Robert Amey.

The role of the judge in his summary is to explain the law. He told the jury, "You are not concerned with the other offenses which are included in it, but when a person is committing these offenses and he uses a weapon or has it upon his person during the time he commits or attempts to commit the offence, or during or at the time of his flight after committing the offence, and death ensues as a consequence, this is murder."

Furlong added, "The jury has to consider whether Young used or had a weapon on his person during the time he committed the offence or during the time he was fleeing after committing the offence. You have got to be satisfied that death ensued as a consequence."

Furlong explained: "Capital murder is the charge against the accused. The law says that murder is capital murder in respect of any person when such a person by his own act caused or assisted in causing the death of a police officer

acting in the course of his duties. So now gentlemen, you
have those two things before you. You have the use of a
weapon and the weapon being on the person of the accused
man when he was attempting flight. You have death being
caused by the use of that weapon during an escape, and while
resisting unlawful arrest. The law says that the killing of a
police officer is in itself proof of intent."

Dealing with the possibility of reducing the charge to
manslaughter, Furlong noted, "There has to be evidence that
a reasonable person can say reduces the offence from the
major one to the less major one. There is no question in this
case because the person killed is a police officer.If you accept
the fact that the final discharge of the gun was accidental, it
doesn't excuse him from being found guilty of the grave
charge for which he stands trial today."

The jury deliberated for almost three hours and returned
with a guilty verdict with a recommendation for clemency.
Young was sentenced to hang on July 15, 1965. Aylward
made an unsuccessful attempt to have the Supreme Court of
Appeal overturn the decision. Justice Furlong had resched-
uled the execution date to October 15 to allow time for an
appeal. Once the appeal was over, the appeal judges set a
new execution date for November 18, 1965. On November 14,
just days before Young was to be hanged, the Federal Cabinet
commuted all death sentences of all prisoners on death row
to life imprisonment.

Young's three accomplices each received three years in
jail.

August 8, 1968

Murdered on Prince of Wales Street

A carnival atmosphere prevailed throughout the city of St. John's on Thursday, August 8, 1968. It was Regatta Day, a civic holiday. The city seemed deserted. While thousands enjoyed the holiday by going to the country, more than 20,000 citizens went to Quidi Vidi Lake in the City's east end.

Among the crowd at Quidi Vidi was thirty-three-year-old Gerard Parsons. Ironically, Parsons' luck in winning a hunting knife at the Regatta would five hours later spell tragedy for his girlfriend Audrey Ballett . In a fit of rage he savagely butchered the girl he had hoped to marry.

This was a story of love at first sight. Parsons met Audrey on Easter Sunday, 1965 and instantly fell in love with her. He was especially proud when she appeared on stage in St. John's in the musical production of *Oliver*.

However, it soon became apparent to Audrey that Gerard had deep emotional problems. He suffered from alcoholism and bouts of depression. When Audrey left Newfoundland, Parsons' emotional state worsened. He made several suicide attempts and was admitted to the Hospital for Mental and Nervous Diseases on two occasions. Upon his release, doctors prescribed the drug Librium to treat his anxiety problems.

On Regatta Day, August 8, Audrey Ballett returned to St. John's and left a message with Mrs. Parsons that she was going to the Races and would drop up to see Gerard at supper time. Gerard was elated. He decided to book off sick from his job at CN and go to the Regatta to meet Audrey. He had taken

four Librium and consumed two beers by the time he got to
Quidi Vidi Lake.

After two hours of unsuccessfully searching for Audrey
he returned home. Audrey called and said she was going to
visit a friend at the Grace and would see him later. At
eight-fifteen p.m. Audrey and her girlfriend were at the
Parsons' home on Prince of Wales Street. Mrs. Parsons and
Audrey's friend left the house to allow the couple some time
alone together.

Two hours later Mrs. Parsons returned with a friend to a
house in darkness. When she turned on the lights she saw
Audrey in a pool of blood on the living room floor. She
screamed, "Audrey! Audrey! My God, she's got her throat
cut!" Her friend called the police.

While the police investigated the murder scene, Parsons
made his getaway in a taxi operated by Ted Hollihan. Several
hours later, when police circulated a description of Parsons
among city cab drivers, Ted Hollihan informed them that he
had taken a man to Flatrock who fitted the description of the
suspect. On Friday, August 9, Head Constable Nick Shanna-
han obtained an arrest warrant for Gerard Parsons. A manhunt involving all available police officers began. All cars
entering and leaving Flatrock were searched, but the suspect
evaded the manhunt for five days. Meanwhile, police at the
murder scene determined that the victim had struggled with
her attacker. There was blood in the hallway and on the
outside area of the house and furniture had been turned over.

Parsons was from the Flatrock area and knew it well.
However, on Monday August 12 at ten-twenty a.m. Constable Everet Carrol arrested Gerard Parsons near Flatrock. He
was wearing the same clothes he had worn the night of the
murder. The suspect did not resist arrest.

During the five-day manhunt the police refused to co-operate with the media. This drew strong criticism from the *Evening Telegram*. An editorial in that paper suggested the police handling of the investigation was instrumental in the fugitive eluding arrest for five days. It stated, "The actions of the St. John's police, probably only laughable in simple matters like parking tickets, can be highly dangerous when a serious crime is committed. The murder of a young woman on Thursday night is a case in point." It continued, "It was as if every action of the police was designed to give the wanted person more time to escape or to commit another crime." The editorial claimed the police refused to confirm that a person was being sought, refused to give a description of the suspect and behaved generally as if the news media were interfering in the pursuit of justice by asking questions.

An assessment at the Hospital for Mental and Nervous Diseases concluded that Parsons was fit to stand trial. The Grand Jury System was in place at the time. Under this system the accused went first to a preliminary hearing, which decided if enough evidence to be referred to the Grand Jury. The Grand Jury then decided whether a case would go to trial. Gerard Parsons was committed to stand trial, and the trial got underway on November 18, 1968 at Supreme Court in St. John's.

Robert Wells defended Parsons and Jim Power represented the Crown before Judge Robert S. Furlong. Crown evidence showed that a violent struggle had taken place and the girl valiantly defended herself. The attack started on the verandah and the victim was dragged back into the house. Sixty-four wounds were inflicted on her body. She received fourteen wounds on the right arm and hand as she attempted to fight off her attacker. Blood was found outside and inside the house. The stove in the hall was knocked out of place.

During the testimony of Pathologist Dr. Young Rho, a

spectator in court fainted. Rho described the 64 knife wounds which penetrated the neck, chest, abdomen, thighs, hands and arm. The fatal wounds in the chest penetrated the heart, stomach and liver.

Police witness Constable Wm. Taylor, told the court that after Parsons was arrested he was placed in the police car. He had a note in which he confessed to the attack and accepted full blame. However, Taylor noted, he seemed not to be aware that Audrey had died. When Constable Taylor testified that Parsons confessed to the killing after receiving the police caution, Wells objected. He argued that the accused was in no condition to understand the caution due to living five days in the open. Judge Furlong conducted a Voire Dire* into the issue and concluded that the confession was admissible. In another verbal confession to Constable Art Pike, Parsons confessed to stabbing the girl and said that she was breathing heavily when he left. He was too frightened to call for help and thought his mother would call for an ambulance when she returned home.

Robert Wells called Dr. Fraser Walsh, psychiatrist at HMND to explain the effects of alcohol and drugs when consumed together. Dr. Walsh told the court that "anyone combining the drug Librium and alcohol over a long period of time would expect anything to happen."

Defence lawyer Wells asked the jury to consider that on the day of the murder, Parsons was irrational and not aware of what he had done. He suggested that his client was guilty of manslaughter, not capital murder.

James Power argued that "Parsons' behaviour before

---

* Legal argument during which the jury is excluded from the courtroom.

August 8 makes no difference. All that matters are the things he did on the evening of August 8. Parsons' story of not remembering events was completely self serving. It was not alcohol that killed Audrey Ballett. It was Gerard Parsons." He asked the jury to convict Parsons on the charge of non-capital murder.

The jury deliberated for six hours and returned a verdict of "not guilty as charged but guilty of manslaughter." Although the maximum penalty for this crime was twenty years, the judge sentenced Gerard Parsons to fourteen years.

June 15, 1976

Child Kidnapped

In June, 1976, the fourteen-year-old daughter of John Craig Eaton — of Eaton's Canada Ltd. — was rescued from a kidnapping attempt by a Newfoundland member of the Toronto Metropolitan Police. During the dramatic confrontation with the kidnapper, Constable Shawn Clarke put his own life on the line.

This life or death situation for Clarke and young Signy Eaton began in the early morning hours of June 15, 1976. Constable Clarke, a tall powerfully built man, was on general police duties with his partner Constable David Linney that day. At one-fifty-four a.m. they responded to what seemed to be a routine call, to check on a complaint of a prowler in the area of the Eaton residence.

Clarke later explained, "It was a routine call...usually nothing happens, but we hurried to the area to check it out." While proceeding to the Eaton home Clarke speculated the prowler was likely someone out getting night worms for a fishing trip. Toronto has a city by-law prohibiting picking of worms at night in city parks. Because of this, people looking for fishing bait frequently go out at night and search neighbour's lawns.

The two officers received a second call on their police radio which convinced Clarke the prowler was just someone looking for worms. The call noted that a neighbour said he saw a man with a hat, a flashlight and a stick walking near the Eaton home.

Within minutes the police pulled into the Eaton driveway and using their flashlights immediately initiated a search of the grounds. Constable Clarke commented, "I checked the back of the residence and my partner checked the front. Everything seemed OK. We were about to leave when I decided to speak to the people in the house, and make sure they were alright."

After unsuccessfully trying to get an answer at the front door, the twenty-four-year-old Newfoundlander walked to the back of the house. Glancing toward a side window he noticed a flashlight in one of the bedrooms. He approached the back door and found it open. Instinctively Clarke sensed something was wrong.

Calmly, Clarke asked his partner to call for a back-up. Meanwhile, he decided to enter the house through the basement door in an effort to prevent any intruder from leaving the house. Constable Clarke described what happened: "I opened the basement door and saw a man standing three feet away from me...holding onto a young girl." The kidnapper was pointing a high-powered military rifle (an M-1 carbine) directly at the Newfoundlander's chest.

Clarke drew his thirty-eight revolver from its holster but the kidnapper ordered him to drop the weapon. Clarke later recalled that though the basement was dark, the man knew Clarke had a gun. Twice the kidnapper demanded Clarke drop his gun, but the cop held his ground.

Constable Clarke said, "I was thinking about the girl's life so I couldn't fire." Instead he kept his revolver pointed at the intruder and slowly backed out of the basement. Outside he pressed against the side of the house. Meanwhile the kidnapper emerged and dropped the girl as he stepped outside the house. She ran back inside the house. Clarke sensed that the kidnapper was only concerned with escape. When he made a dash across the yard, Clarke followed in hot pursuit. The kidnapper clutched his rifle as he ran.

Clarke fired six bullets at the kidnapper. It was dark and each shot missed. Clarke said, "He got over a fence and I could hear his footsteps so I continued the pursuit."

The constable ordered a four block area to be sealed off and the Emergency Tactical Force was called in to assist. By dawn the police had forty-seven-year-old Ernest Carron of Montreal in custody for the kidnapping attempt. Carron was turned over to Constable Clarke, who took him to the police station for questioning.

When police investigators returned to the Eaton mansion to search for clues they were surprised by what they found. In an upstairs bedroom, the intruder had confined thirty-nine-year-old John Eaton and his wife Sherry.

When Carron first entered the house he took John and Sherry at gunpoint to the upstairs room. There he tied and gagged his captives. He then searched the house until he found the Eatons young daughter, Signy. Pointing the gun at her he threatened to shoot if she did not do as she was told. He was in the final stage of his crime, leaving the house with his victim, when his scheme was thwarted by the Newfoundland police officer.

Clarke had had a long-time ambition to be a police officer. He tried to join both the RCMP and the Royal Newfoundland Constabulary but was not accepted. He then applied to the Toronto Metropolitan Police and earned a place on the force. At the time of the kidnapping attempt Clarke had punched in two years on the force, and this marked the first occasion on which he had to use his gun. The life threatening confrontation with danger did not dampen his spirit or love for police work. He commented, "This is one job that I put in one hundred per cent effort and I enjoy every shift."

February 2, 1976
The Murder of Mona Johnson

The macabre slaying of forty-nine year old Mona Johnson at Little Catalina shocked her neighbours and friends. The trial of her killer absolutely amazed them. Newfoundlanders have rarely been subjected to such a ghastly and despicable a crime; our courts have rarely seen such a bizarre murder trial as the one that followed.

This tragic story began to unfold at two a.m. February 4, 1976, when the Volunteer Fire Brigade at Little Catalina responded to a fire at the home of Mona Johnson. The fire burned until six-thirty a.m. and completely destroyed the residence. Searching the ruins, police discovered the body of Mona Johnson and immediately concluded she had been murdered. There was a plastic wire around her wrists and throat and her body was partially nude.

The RCMP began to question people in the community. Their first stop was the home of Anne Chaulk, where Mona had lived for awhile after being divorced. Chaulk's grandson, Andrew Scott Reid, told police he had been near Mona Johnson's house at one a.m. and saw a dark coloured car parked in her driveway.

The investigation continued with police talking to others until the information they gathered led them back to Andrew Scott Reid. This time Reid told investigators he had been drinking with friends until one a.m. when they dropped him off near Mona's. He claimed he saw a car in the driveway and didn't bother to go in. When police asked to see the clothes he had been wearing and requested an explanation as to how he got the scratch on his nose, his mood changed and he asked to use the phone.

He then changed his story and admitted he had visited Mona's house. Reid described to the police the first of several bizarre accounts of what happened there that night. He claimed he saw an old girlfriend named Rose, with his baby in her arms. According to his poice statement, when he asked her if she still loved him, she pushed a shoe horn down the child's throat and replied, "Here's how much I love you." Enraged, he strangled her and set her clothes on fire. Reid finished his story by asserting that he got the scratch on his nose while playing with his dog. The story suggested that Reid may have been hallucinating from drug or alcohol abuse and while in this state killed Mona Johnson.

Later that day, while being given a polygraph test, Reid broke down and confessed to killing Mona Johnson. He told police he put the clothes he wore down an old toilet and he denied having had sex with the victim. During the drive to the Bonavista RCMP officer Reid said, "I had to get rid of her. I took the cord off the telephone. I cut it with a knife. I hit her. There was blood all over the place. There was blood on my clothes. I knew I had to get rid of her. When I tied her up I didn't think she was dead but she didn't move. I got the wire and tied it around her neck to make sure she was dead."

The trial got underway on June 14, 1976. The twenty-six-year-old fish plant worker sat quietly throughout the trial and glanced occasionally at his wife. He took notes during the proceedings. The Crown was represented by Barry Hill and Reid was defended by Robert Wells.

The prosecutor told the court he would present evidence to show that Reid had gagged, bound, sexually assaulted and then strangled Mona Johnson. He then set fire to the house in an attempt to destroy the evidence.

The defence attempted to block admission of five statements (three written and two oral) Reid had given Police. However, after a Voir Dire which lasted several days, all statements were admitted.

The only witness called by the defence was the defendant.

The autopsy showed that the victim had been badly beaten and strangled. The report revealed that plastic coated telephone wire was used and the victim had been gagged, beaten, raped and strangled. Death had been caused by strangulation. The fire as cause of death was ruled out because there was no soot in the victim's lungs.

Crime lab experts testified that Mona Johnson's blood stains were found on Reid's clothing. Sgt. John Neill told the court that during the polygraph test Reid broke down and confessed to the murder. He testified, "Reid was crouched in his chair in a bent over fetal position, grasping both of his arms. He had his feet underneath his chair in a defensive position. There were outward signs of nervousness and he was stammering." Reid passed out during the test.

Evidence at trial showed that Reid had been at Mona Johnson's at the time of the murder and he was in good shape when dropped off by friends. A neighbour told the court that she looked out her window at four-thirty a.m. and saw Reid throwing something into an outhouse.

The defence called its only witness, Andrew Scott Reid. He was remarkably cool and in control. Reid's account of the murder now bore no resemblance to his description of being outraged at the sight of an old girlfriend pushing a shoehorn down the child's throat. It also contradicted the confession he had given the police during the polygraph. In court, he testified that the victim was his cousin. He described his visit to her home that night. He said, "I knocked. there was no answer. I walked in. The kitchen was dark. The next thing I knew I was knocked to the floor by someone. I was pinned partially face down and I heard voices saying, 'Hurry up, we got to get out of here. We got to get out of the province tonight.' Then a man with dark hair and wearing a brown leather jacket came on the scene. He rushed into the bedroom while the other man had me pinned to the floor. He returned from the room with something in his hand. He pushed what seemed to be clothing in my face and there was something wet on it. The man holding me said, 'Hurry, light the fire.' I then saw the flickering light of flame from the bedroom. He shouted, 'Let's get out of here.'"

Reid claimed the men threatened to kill his whole family if he told anyone what happened. He said he tried to help the victim but when he noticed the wire around her neck he became frightened and ran home.

In his summation, Robert Wells argued that the Crown had not proven its case. He suggested that their case was based on the theory that the accused visited Johnson for sex. However, the evidence had not clearly shown that the accused did have sex with the victim. He stressed that at no time in talking with the police did the accused admit to having sex with the victim.

Barry Hill felt the evidence spoke strongly for the guilt of the accused. He argued that, "It's an insult to the intelligence of everyone here. Never before have you been subjected to such an arrogant story. Andrew Reid went to Mona Johnson's for sex, and the sexual portion of the crime was too repulsive for him to admit."

In his address to the Jury, Judge Mifflin stated,"This was a horrible and horrendous crime." He flatly told the jury he did not believe the testimony of Andrew Reid. However, he explained, while it is not unusual for a trial judge to express his opinion on the evidence, "You the jury are in no way bound to abide by my opinion.Reid's testimony is too ridiculous to talk about"

The jury's deliberation was short. In just 80 minutes they returned with a guilty verdict. The conviction carried a mandatory life sentence.

When the sentence was read out in court, Reid and his wife broke into tears.Viola Reid was escorted from the courthouse by friends. As Andrew Scott Reid was escorted from the courtroom he lost consciousness and stumbled. A short while later he was on his feet and led from the room to begin serving his life sentence.

Chapter Six

Justice Potpourri

Hangmen and Executioners

In 1922, W.A. Doyle of Verdun, Quebec, offered to come to Newfoundland and act as executioner at the hanging of Wo Fen Game in St. John's for a fee of one hundred dollars plus expenses. Wo had been found guilty of the triple slaying of three fellow Chinese laundrymen on Carter's Hill and had been sentenced to be hanged on December 16, 1922. Doyle's offer was turned down, possibly because of an execution he bungled at Woodstock, New Brunswick on September 25 that year.

On that occasion, Doyle, an experienced hangman, turned up at the New Brunswick prison with a strong smell of liquor on his breath. He was there to execute a man named Bennie Swimm for the murder of his sweetheart. The deputy sheriff noticed the executioner staggering as he walked up the gallows. The prisoner was brought to the scaffold, death rites given, and Doyle placed the rope around his neck.

Doyle pulled the lever, the trap door opened, and the prisoner dropped. The prison doctor was in the process of examining the prisoner when Doyle ordered his assistant F.G. Gill to cut him down. When the doctor protested, Doyle said, "He's deader than a door nail." At this point the deputy-sheriff interceded and ordered Doyle away from the scaffold.

The doctor was allowed to complete his examination and discovered that Swimm's neck was not broken and he was still breathing. Three doctors watched over Swimm for thirty minutes as his pulse got stronger. The sheriff reminded those present that the court order stated that the prisoner was to be hanged "until dead," and since he was not yet dead they were left no other choice but to bring him back to the gallows. Swimm, only half-conscious, was carried back to the plat-form and a successful execution was performed by Doyle's assistant, Mr. Gill.

Newfoundland Justice officials decided to decline Doyle's offer and recruit a local but inexperienced man to execute Wo Fen Game. They found a willing executioner in the person of a Bell Island man serving a term for bestiality at Her Majesty's Penitentiary. The prisoner's term was reduced in exchange for agreeing to act as executioner. The prisoner-executioner bungled the hanging. The rope was too short and caused Fen Game to suffer strangulation instead of instant death. His neck was not dislocated and he dangled on the rope, kicking and squirming, for several minutes.

There have been other bungled executions at the prison in St. John's. In the hanging of William Parnell, an inexperi-enced executioner allowed too much rope, and Parnell, who was overweight, was nearly decapitated when he fell through the trap door.

The last hanging to take place in Newfoundland was that of Herbert Spratt for the murder of Josephine O'Brien in 1942. That executioner was professional and Spratt died instantly. On that occasion the executioner was brought in from the mainland. He checked in at Hotel Newfoundland and carried a leather briefcase containing his own hanging rope. The executioner was a very short man and had to stand on a stool in order to place the rope around the prisoner's neck. When the trap door opened, Spratt fell, and his neck was dislocated causing instant death.

The history of the gallows in Canada is filled with examples of bungled executions. In 1831 an inexperienced hangman used the wrong kind of rope in executing Cornelius Burry for the murder of a policeman. When Burry was dropped from the gallows, the rope broke. He got back on his feet and, with the black hood over his head and the hanging rope trailing from his neck, walked around in a daze. Guards quickly seized him and escorted him back to the scaffold where he was again hanged, this time successfully.

On June 18, 1839 the execution of Pierre Narbonne, who was being hanged for participating in rebellion, turned into a spectacle of horror. Narbonne's stump arm slipped from the rope which bound his arms together after he had plummeted through the trap door. When his good arm worked free he grabbed the hanging rope and pulled himself back onto the scaffold. However, each time he made it the sheriff shoved him back. Finally, he wrestled with the sheriff, and two guards had to assist the sheriff into throwing him back into the jaws of the gallows. Despite his struggle, he died of strangulation.

In British Columbia in the late nineteenth century an old sick Indian had to be carried to the gallows and hanged while sitting in his chair. A year later his son confessed to the murder for which his father had been executed.

On September 12, 1919 at Bordeaux Jail, Quebec, the executioner took one and a half hours to hang Antonio Sprecage, who had been convicted of murder. Finally he went into convulsions and died of strangulation. At Calgary, Alberta on February 17, 1914 a man named Jack Holmes, too sick to stand, was brought to the gallows in a chair. When the doctors examined his body after it was cut down and still tied into the chair, they discovered he was still alive. He died fifteen minutes later of suffocation. Although he was dead, the sheriff had him brought back to the gallows and again he was hanged. This was necessary because the court order stated he was to be hanged by the neck until dead and the sheriff felt the order had not been carried out.

The most difficult person to execute in Canadian history was no doubt the six-foot, 275 pound Marie Anne Crispen who had been sentenced to hang for the murder of her lover's wife. On the morning of her execution, the hangman, followed by two female attendants, walked into her cell to prepare her for the gallows. Crispen, who dwarfed the executioner in size, punched him in the face and knocked him partially unconscious. Guards brought her under control but she broke away and began tossing the guards out through the cell door. She was outnumbered and the execution was completed. However, the prison staff sported bruises and black eyes for days afterwards.

The Many Methods of Execution

To execute a person instantly and efficiently by hanging requires experience and expertise in technique. Before the last half of the nineteenth century, people who went to the gallows usually died from strangulation. The man responsible for improving the hanging methods was the British hangman, William Marwood, known as "the scientific hangman." Marwood succeeded William Calcraft, the most famous of

British hangmen, and Marwood immediately set out to make hangings more humane. He had noticed that the short drop used by Calcraft, and the one-and-a-half inch diameter rope, caused strangulation. He chose a softer, pliable three-quarter-inch rope and stretched it using bags of cement before trying it on condemned prisoners. He added to this the procedure known as the long drop. He determined that the heavier the weight, the shorter the drop should be. This prevented decapitation. John Burry, a police officer who succeeded Marwood, was the first to work out a list of tables according to the weight of the prisoner.

By the end of the nineteenth century the English recognized the need for professional executions to ensure that hanging would be a humane form of execution. In response to this need, a special training program was instituted for hangmen and kept secret from the public. To be accepted one had to be of the highest character and discreet. The training consisted of pinioning a dummy figure of a man in the condemned cell, escorting him to the gallows and at a given signal pulling the lever which opened the trap door. Students also learned the type of rope and the drop schedule. Many students lost their nerve and quit. John Ellis, the uncle of Canada's most famous executioner Arthur Ellis, was a graduate of the secret hanging school.

Arthur learned the trade from his uncle. During his career as an executioner, Arthur Ellis executed over 600 people in England, Middle East and Canada. Unlike many other executioners Ellis believed in capital punishment, but was opposed to hanging. He said, "Hanging belongs to a past age. I am strongly in favour of the electric chair, not only on the grounds of humanity, but it is safer in every way and it is instantaneous." He added, "I consider it the most sacred calling any man could have, since I am entrusted with carrying out the highest sentence our courts can pass."

Another famous Canadian hangman was John Radclieve, who learned his trade under Marwood and executed 200 people during his career. Because he was known as a hangman, his family left him. He continued with the job because he believed if he was doing wrong, then the Government of Canada was doing wrong. Eventually he quit, saying, "The remorse which comes over me is terrible and my nerves give out until I have not slept days at a time. I am two hundred times a murderer but I won't kill another man."

One of the most unusual methods of hanging was the one developed and used by Radclieve. Just as Calcraft had made his mark in history by improving pinioning methods, and Marwood by developing the long drop, Radclieve hoped his method would earn him recognition in gallows history. It seems he paid much attention to the difficult time condemned men had in walking up to the Gallows. He sought a way to eliminate the steps altogether. His method was a drastic change from traditional hangings. When it was first used at a hanging in Toronto, witnesses were surprised to see no platform or steps, just three pieces of 6' by 6' by 14 feet timber, two embedded upright into the ground and about six feet apart, and the third beam was placed across these. This top bar extended six feet out over the upright and was fourteen feet from the ground.

Radclieve was invited to use his new method for the execution of a man named Kene who had murdered his wife in Toronto. At the execution site, Kene was taken directly to the ground beneath the hanging ropes. The rope was placed around his neck and carried over the beam, where it was attached to an iron weight about four hundred pounds. Kane had been placed a little off-centre so that when the bolt was pulled releasing the weight, the rope jerked Kane sideways and straight up. This action caused immediate dislocation of the neck and death was instantaneous. The success of the method resulted in Radclieve being assigned to execute several others. These were all clean and death was quick.

However, a horrifying spectacle resulted in 1890 when he executed Reginald Birchall. Radclieve pulled the rope to release the bolt. The hanging rope slipped to the front of Birchall's face and failed to dislocate his neck. The result was a bloody and slow strangulation which lasted eighteen minutes. Radclieve's method was used only once after that, then abandoned. Authorities felt it was effective but too gruesome for witnesses.

While many Canadian executioners revelled in their notoriety as executioners to the point of having pictures taken and soliciting business, Newfoundland hangmen were the opposite. They shunned notoriety, wore masks and concealed their identities.

The grotesque forms of execution methods like quartering, boiling in oil, burning alive have given way to newer forms considered more humane. But are they really? Even these newer forms have their grisly aspects. Even when a prisoner is executed by a professional, and death is instantaneous, it is a harrowing experience for family and friends who view the body. The eyes are popped almost out of the victim's head, the tongue swollen and protruding from the mouth and the rope tears the flesh from the face.

In most electric chairs two electrodes with sponge faces soaked in salt water are attached to the prisoner, one to his head and the other to the calf of his leg. The electrodes are moistened to assure good conductivity and to reduce the burning of the flesh. Usually 2200 volts of electricity are used, driving the body temperature to 138 degrees. When the current strikes the victim, first he is pitched forward in the chair. There is a buzzing and crackling sound of current and the skin turns red. Sometimes sparks shoot from the electrodes. A wisp of grey or white smoke rises from the top of the head and the leg where the electrodes are attached. this is caused by the drying out of the sponge. There is the added horror of the smell of burning flesh.

Lethal gas is not as terrible as either hanging or electricity but also has its horrors. There is no mutilation of the body involved in a gas execution. The prisoner is strapped into a metal chair and a stethoscope attached to him or her. The door of the execution chamber is then sealed. At a signal from the Warden, the executioner presses a lever that releases cyanide pellets into a container of distilled water and sulphuric acid. At first the eyes almost pop out, then they turn purple and there is extreme evidence of pain and strangling.

Only the state of Utah gives a prisoner the choice of being shot or hanged. If a prisoner is hanged, three pieces of rope are released at the same time one by each of three executioners. Only one of these releases the mechanism to the trap door. If a prisoner is shot, five men from the firing squad shoot but only four of the five use real bullets.

Lawyers

*T*he role of lawyer in the justice system developed slowly from a non-paying position into a profession. Initially, it was illegal for a lawyer to accept fees for his services. To offer money to a lawyer for advice was the same as offering money to a jury member. The lawyer's role was as clerk and interpreter for the court. His responsibility was to help the client present his case to the judge in an expeditious and intelligible form.

Origins of term 'Admitted to the Bar'

The term 'admitted to the Bar' originated from the usage of an actual bar in English courtrooms. A bar ran across the room to separate the claimants from the judge or judges. The judge often invited his friends to sit beside him and watch the court in action. At the close of court, he would order a portion of grog be given to all present. The grog was passed over the bar by the barrister.

The idea of distributing rum in the courtroom was to send everyone away happy and to prove that the judge acted without prejudice. When a young man was admitted to the Bar it meant he could approach the Bar and say things to the judge who sat behind it.

If a lawyer tried to influence the court by holding back evidence, or by emphasizing certain facts to the exclusion of others, it was considered a misdemeanour. His role was simply to assist the court.

Eventually, so many barristers were accused of accepting bribes or taking fees that it was arranged for each barrister to have a pocket on the back of his gown. This has been described as a portable poor box and was located between the shoulders where he could not reach it. In that way, if a client wished to show his gratitude by dropping something in the pocket, he could do so. However, the barrister would not know anything about this until the court adjourned and he had removed the gown.

Magistrates

During the late eighteenth century, magistrates in New-foundland felt they needed a larger income. To accommodate them, authorities taxed the 108 taverns in St. John's. Each establishment was required to pay four and a half guineas. Half of this amount went to the three local justices while the remaining half went into public funds. Fines were also a means of income for magistrates.

Judgement Recovery

A man named O'Driscoll of Bay Bulls earned the distinction of being the only poor man to recover money through our court system from a merchant, during the eighteenth century.

O'Driscoll was downhearted when the courts had delivered a judgement against him. The loss meant ruin for this proud fisherman. One day O'Driscoll was discussing his problems with a friend near the wharf at Bay Bulls. His Irish friend pointed to a man off a British vessel nearby and suggested, "Ask him to plead your case again and bedad, you will win before the ould judge."

O'Driscoll, feeling he had nothing to lose, approached the man and requested his help. The Englishman was a jolly good natured sort of fellow and he accepted the challenge. He accompanied the poor fisherman to the court and succeeded in obtaining a judgement favourable to his client. Only after the trial did the fisherman learn that he had been represented by Prince William Henry IV of England. At the time the prince was in Newfoundland as captain of the HMS *Pegasus*.

Problems with Witnesses

Prior to the 1730s there were major problems involved in enforcing the law in Newfoundland. Apprehension of the criminal was diffiuclt enough, but getting him or her to trial and obtaining a conviction was a major problem. This was due to the system which required that all persons arrested on criminal charges had to be sent to England for trial at local expense. In addition, witnesses were also required to make the trip. Although the witnesses' expenses were paid to England, once the trial was over they were responsible for their own expenses which included accommodations, food, and transportation back to Newfoundland.

In addition, witnesses would have to give up part or all of the fishing or farming season in order to appear at trial. Understandably witnesses were hard to find and therefore criminals were infrequently brought to justice.

There was an improvement in the justice system in 1729. Governor Henry Osbourne became the first governor for Newfoundland with authority to appoint justices. Fishing Admirals were replaced by navy officers, who acted as judges in the summertime. When the naval fleet returned to England in the fall, local people were appointed to take their place.

Most of those appointed were illiterate and knew little about law. One such judge was John Stripling, a tavern owner. In one case tried by Stripling and three other judges, the defendant was found guilty of being drunk and swearing in public. He was ordered to pay a $750 fine — an enormous amount in those days. Stripling and his colleagues divided the entire fine among themselves. Not a penny went to the Crown. The poor had little chance in these courts. Judges were paid a fee for each trial, plus a percentage of the fines collected, and if a person couldn't pay a fine he went to jail.

Penitentiary Conditions 1859-1932

*F*rom the opening of Her Majesty's Penitentiary in St. John's in 1859 until 1932, conditions at the prison were very severe. Rehabilitation of the criminal was not a consideration. Instead, authorities relied on punishment as the only means of changing a criminal's behaviour and deterring others from committing criminal acts. John Fagan, a former Superintendent of HMP described conditions, saying, "The sheer hardship, deprivation, humiliation and physical punishment associated with imprisonment were relied upon to reform the criminal and deter him from future behaviour."

Juveniles caught breaking the law were sentenced to the penitentiary. Upon being admitted they were given six strokes with a birch rod and the same punishment was administered before being released.

The humiliation for prisoners began on the first day at HMP. Immediately after entering they were given close-cropped haircuts and this condition was maintained until the prisoner was released. Fagan noted there were hygienic reasons for doing this but the underlying purpose was to punish and humiliate. Another means of humiliating the criminal was the type of prison clothing wore. The garb consisted of a jumper and trousers. The trousers were made from black and white materials with each pair of trousers divided vertically, half white and half black. This design also served to discourage escapes and facilitate the recapture of runaway prisoners. This practice was extremely humiliating, especially for those on work details outside the prison.

The prison menu was another source of punishment. For the first two weeks the diet consisted only of hard bread and water. The bread and water menu improved after two weeks. Daily breakfast consisted of porridge with molasses and black tea sweetened with molasses. There was no variation of the breakfast menu.

The noonday meal on Monday, Wednesday and Friday was fish and potatoes, black tea and hard bread. On Sunday, Tuesday, Thursday and Saturday the main meal consisted of pea soup, rice soup or boiled beans, black tea and hard bread.

There were two diets used at the penitentiary. One was for prisoners doing less than three months while the second was for those doing more than three months. The difference became apparent on the four days when soup or beans were served. Inmates doing more than three months received four ounces of meat with their soup or beans, while the short-term prisoners received no meat whatsoever during their term.

Supper consisted of black tea sweetened with molasses, and hard bread. Like breakfast, there was no variation in the supper menu. Each inmate received a daily ration of nine cakes of hard bread which had to last for the day. Soft bread and butter was a real treat and was only given on the recommendation of the prison physician.

When a prisoner was delivered to the penitentiary by the constabulary he was given a mattress sack and enough straw to stuff it with. The inmate also had to sew up the other end. His bed consisted of a wooden pallet built six inches above the floor. Neither the staff nor inmates were permitted to smoke.

No recreation of any kind was allowed and newspapers, radios and movies were taboo. As a health measure only, all inmates were allowed half an hour daily in the open air during which time they were permitted to walk around in a circle in the prison yard. There was a weekly medical clinic and dental treatment was limited to teeth extractions.

It wasn't until 1931 that a more humane approach was adopted at the prison, when a day school with a full-time teacher was opened at the penitentiary. During the first year sixty-seven students participated in the project. Commenting on the problems of educating prisoners, the teacher said, "In this school we have the lack of education, no home life and poor environment and it is a big job to try in a few months to undo the killing influence of years."

On alternate days a thirty minute talk was given to inmates of the penitentiary. They were told that the keys to golden opportunities included knowing how to act properly in public and being able to remember good manners.

The harsh discipline and practices were abolished or modified and by the mid-thirties an improved diet scale was introduced, black and white uniforms disappeared and close-cropped hair-cuts were no longer mandatory. Corporal punishment was abolished.

Early Newfoundland Justice

The eighteenth and nineteenth centuries in Newfoundland could be referred to as the era of gallows, rogues and branding irons. Public gallows were constructed throughout the island by orders of Governor Bonfoy as a constant reminder and deterrent to those contemplating the criminal life. For crimes other than capital offenses there were stocks, pillars, whirley-gigs, branding irons and the cat o' nine tails.

The Courthouse in St. John's had its own branding iron. This punishment was normally administered in court in the presence of judges and witnesses. A prisoner sentenced to be branded had his right arm strapped into an iron device to assure he couldn't move it. An officer designated by the court readied the branding iron by leaving it in the open fireplace until it was burning red. The prisoner was told the iron would be pressed against the palm of his hand for as long as it took him to say three times, as fast as he could, "God save the King." The letter R meant rogue and would be used to identify a repeat offender.

The pillory was a wooden frame into which the ankles, wrists and neck were inserted, confining the prisoner for a period set by the Court. The stocks were similar, but restricted only the ankles of the prisoner. Public flogging was common. The instruments used for this included the birch rod, the whip and the cat o' nine tails. The cat consisted of a wooden handle with nine leather straps, each strap with nine knots in it.

Sometimes the prestige given judges, some of who were barely literate, went to their heads. Tom Warden, Justice of the Peace at Trinity, found himself in court after being accused of assaulting the wife of John Barnes. Mrs. Barnes failed to address His Worship in a proper manner, so His Worship picked up a piece of wood and struck her with it. He was found guilty and ordered to pay five pounds sterling in damages to Mrs. Barnes. Warden was also ordered to construct at his own expense, a whirley-gig for the punishment of turbulent and disorderly women. This was a form of punishment in which a woman was placed in a cage on an axis. The cage was then turned, continuously spinning for a period of time designated by the court.

In another case the surrogate magistrate at Harbour Grace once used a very unorthodox method to deal with a Harbour Main fisherman who had a history of exploiting and physically abusing his employees. The magistrate gave permission for the victim to beat the daylights out of his employer.

Considering the harsh penalties handed down in Newfoundland Courts during the 18th and 19th centuries, one might conclude that our early justice system was harsh. However, it would be more accurate to say that while criminal penalties were indeed harsh, their application in Newfoundland was generally merciful.

At one period in history there were actually 222 offences in law for which a person could be given the death penalty. These included such offences as: stealing a cow, cutting down a tree on crown land; stealing or killing a rabbit on crown land; rape; blasphemy; harbouring an offender against the revenue act; stealing from a dwelling forty shillings or more, or stealing from a shop five shillings or more. At the beginning of the nineteenth century two hundred such offences were still in force, but by 1823 that number was reduced to one hundred offences. Yet Newfoundland history records less than thirty legal executions.

Elsewhere the hangman was far more active. In a three-month period in London, England, ninety-four people were executed, most of them for crimes other than murder. During the French Revolution one thousand people were executed monthly. In 1820 in London, forty-six people were hanged for forging bank notes. It was later discovered by the authorities that more than half the notes were genuine. In just one day in 1829 in England twenty-four people were executed. Only one of those had committed murder. Closer to home in Halifax, Nova Scotia, twelve people were hanged the same day, all for stealing potatoes.

In Newfoundland, children were not executed. However, age was no barrier elsewhere. The first person executed on mainland Canada was a child of sixteen. Her crime was petty theft. In Quebec a boy of fifteen was hanged for stealing a cow. On September 18, 1803, a thirteen-year-old boy was executed at Montreal for stealing a cow. In England ten children ranging in age from ten to sixteen were hanged on the same day and their bodies left swinging from the gallows as "a warning to men and a spectacle for the angels." Their crime was stealing food because they were hungry. In another case in England a nine-year-old boy was hanged for breaking into a house. Shortly after that execution an eleven-year-old girl and her seven-year-old brother were hanged for stealing food, and a fifteen-year-old girl was hanged for killing her grandfather.

Compared to other places our method of execution was more humane. In Newfoundland the only form of capital punishment was hanging. There were the added punishments of gibbeting (hanging in chains after death) and dissection used in some gruesome crimes in Newfoundland, but these were punishments inflicted after death.

England, France, and the United States sometimes burned people at the stake; England and France used boiling in oil, drowning pits, beheading and pressing to death. Germany, Spain and France used the wheel. This procedure involved strapping the victim to fit the wheel's rim. The executioner used a thick iron bar to systematically break every bone in the victim's body. It was a test of skill to inflict this punishment without breaking the flesh. An improvement in this method was the garrote. The executioner passed a double cord through the spokes of the wheel and around the victim's neck. After breaking the bones he would then pull the cord to strangle the victim so that he would be spared a lingering death.

Italy, as late as the nineteenth century, used the mazzatello, a revolting type of execution to witness. The victim was led up the scaffold where an open coffin awaited him. He stood by the coffin and the executioner banged him over the head once or twice with a mallet the Italians called **mazza or mazzatello.** Following this the executioner drew a knife and cut the victim's throat.

Pressing was a specialty in England, used mainly against those who refused to enter a plea in court. This methods involved loading iron weights on the chest of the victim until he was squashed or pressed to death. Other execution methods involved quartering; this meant tearing the victim to pieces. Each of the victim's limbs was tied to one of four horses and then the four horses driven off in four different directions. There was also spearing to death.

A person found guilty of murdering one person in Newfoundland was given only one death sentence. However, in Montreal, a man who committed two murders was given two death sentences with each sentence being carried out. At first he was tied to a wheel on the scaffold and every bone in his body broken with an iron pipe. Although he was dead, the second capital punishment sentence of hanging had to be enforced. The dead man was removed from the wheel, a noose placed around his neck and then he was hanged.

The penalty for mutiny or high treason was perhaps the most gruesome of capital punishment penalties. A person found guilty of such offenses was dragged to the gallows and not allowed to walk. He was partially hanged, then lowered while still alive. His entrails were then cut out and burnt before his eyes. Water was sometimes thrown in his face to revive him and then the hanging was finished. When he was cut down the executioner cut the head, arms, and legs from the body; parboiled them to preserve them, and then placed them on public display.

While in Newfoundland we did have two cases at least in

which this penalty could have been applied, our courts did not use it. It was certainly a harsh era. On mainland Canada lunatics were sometimes flogged at the public whipping post to drive the devil out.

Considering the times, the number of offenses for which capital punishment could be applied and the barbaric methods of execution available, it seems that while criminal penalties were indeed harsh, their application by Newfoundland courts was generally merciful. Our court justices more often turned to banishment or transportation as a punishment rather than execution.